REPUBLI

BY MARCUS TULLIUS CICERO

TRANSLATED FROM THE LATIN
BY
GEORGE WILLIAM FEATHERSTONHAUGH

Be it remembered, that on the 23d day of January, A. D. 1829, in the fifty-third year of the Independence of the United States of America, G. & C. Carvill, of the said district, hath deposited in this office the title of a book, the right whereof they claim as proprietors, in the words following, to wit:

"The Republic of Cicero, translated from the Latin; and accompanied with a Critical and Historical Introduction. By G. W. Featherstonhaugh, Esq., Fellow of the Geological Society of London; of the American Philosophical Society; of the Lyceum of Natural History of New-York, &c. &c. &c."

In conformity to the Act of Congress of the United States, entitled, "An Act for the encouragement of learning, by securing the copies of maps, charts, and books, to the authors and proprietors of such copies, during the times therein mentioned;" and also, to an Act, entitled, "An Act, supplementary to an Act, entitled an Act for the encouragement of learning, by securing the copies of maps, charts, and books, to the authors and proprietors of such copies, during the times therein mentioned, and extending the benefits thereof to the arts of designing, engraving, and etching historical and other prints."

FRED. I. BETTS,
Clerk of the Southern District of New-York.

TO
RODERICK IMPEY MURCHISON, Esq.
F. R. S., F. G. S., &c. &c. &c.

I dedicate these pages to you, my dear Murchison, that you may have a renewed assurance of my great esteem and friendship for you. I should have had a livelier satisfaction in doing so, if the part I have had in the production of them, were more worthy of your refined taste. I hope to offer some compensation, however, in the assurance, that you will find in them many congenial opinions and principles.

G. W. Featherstonhaugh.
New-York, January 21, 1829.

PREFACE.

I am not aware that any translation of the Republic of Cicero into the English tongue has been made.

Believing that it cannot but excite a deep interest with generous minds, as well on account of the high nature of the subject, the illustrious name of Cicero, as of the great motives which led him to compose this work, I venture to offer a translation of it to the public.

In this extensive republic, where every individual reads, it appears peculiarly proper, that an English dress should be given to a work, of which almost every page teaches that public happiness depends upon individual virtue.

Cicero's definition of a republic, that it is an association of the people for the defence and advancement of the common interest; will be understood here, which may be doubtingly said of any other republics now in existence.

A bare translation of the fragments of this mutilated work, unassisted by any commentary, could not but have been unsatisfactory. The deficiencies of the original are somewhat compensated to us, not alone in the grandeur of thought which pervades it, but in the majesty of diction, precise, elevated, as it frequently is, and always governed by the most refined taste. It would be a vain effort to attempt the dignity of the Latin tongue, when adorned with the elegancies of the Ciceronian style. Humbly as the translation may deserve to be considered, it will perhaps be deemed sufficiently faithful: and that the translator has not altogether failed in pointing out to grave and reflecting minds, the immediate cause of the ruin of a noble Republic.

He has therefore prefixed a brief historical introduction; the which, whether it will be thought too long, or not sufficiently detailed, will probably depend upon the reader's historical recollections. The motive for drawing it up was to render the work more generally useful and acceptable.

INTRODUCTION.

The imperfect manuscript, a translation of which is now presented to the American public, was discovered in the Library of the Vatican, by Professor Angelo Mai; a person of singular ingenuity in the detection of those Palimpsests whose contents were written upon ancient writings partially erased. A fac simile of part of the MSS. accompanies this work. The Republic of Cicero was greatly cherished by those who lived in and near his times; of which occasional evidences are found in the writings of antiquity. But the tyranny of the emperors bridled the Romans so soon after its appearance, that Horace, Virgil, Seneca, Quintilian, Pliny, and even Tacitus, have not dared to praise it, lest they should bring down vengeance upon themselves. It is remarkable that while despotism was rapidly extinguishing philosophy and letters, and the very existence of these precious monuments of better times was scarcely thought of; the Christian religion was gradually raising up amidst the persecutions of the primitive church, new champions for truth and justice; to whose works we are indebted for many valuable fragments of the best writers of antiquity, and for almost all the passages of Cicero's Republic which we were acquainted with, until the late discovery of professor Mai. It is in the works of St. Augustin and of Lactantius that these passages most abound; and they are appealed to by them as most eloquent arguments, in support of just government, and virtuous conduct. Scipio's Dream, forming the only part of the sixth book which has been preserved, and which is one of the most splendid passages that has been saved from antiquity, has long had a place in the works of Macrobius, a writer at the beginning of the fifth century, addicted to the Pythagorean mysticisms; and who has preserved it probably on account of the occult astronomical relation of numbers contained in it. Notwithstanding the mutilated state of the MSS., the order of the books is distinctly preserved, the general plan of the work is obvious, and we have much greater reason to rejoice at what we possess, than to regret what is wanting. The disordered state of the government and the republic at large, evidently suggested to Cicero this patriotic and bold attempt to stem the influence of bad men, and raise the falling liberties of his country. In this highly philosophical discourse he sought to recall the Romans from the interests of ambitious individuals, and fix their attention upon the greater interests of the country, where each man had a stake: to revive their veneration for the simplicity of the early institutions of Rome, and for the men who had made themselves illustrious by their virtues: and to guard the people more effectually against the innovations and factions now succeeding each other with so much rapidity, he invests those ancient times with a perfection, that the attractions of his eloquence alone can excuse.

Of the original simplicity of the government, some evidences are afforded by this work; as where it is stated that lands were assigned to the sovereign, and cultivated for him by the people, that he might have nothing to do but administer justice. The principal men too of the state in those early times lived in the vicinity of Rome, cultivating a small possession. The illustrious names of Fabius, Lentulus, Cicero, &c., were perhaps given to those husbandmen who excelled in the cultivation of those vegetables; such was the opinion of Pliny.[1]

The censor had the power of reprimanding those whose fields were slovenly cultivated. Many customs of those antique times are found in Cato's curious Treatise on Rural Affairs. "Our ancestors constituted and ordained thus in their Laws: A thief was condemned to double restitution; an usurer to quadruple. You may judge from this how much worse a citizen they deemed the usurer to be than the thief. And when they praised a worthy man, they spoke thus of him: 'that he was a good farmer, an excellent husbandman.' He that was commended in these terms, was thought to be praised enough."[2] And again speaking of a good husbandman, he says, "He should part with his old cattle, his weaned calves and lambs, his wool, his skins, his old carts and worn out irons, his old slaves, and his sick ones; and if he has got any thing else he does not want, let him sell it. A father of a family ought always to sell and never to buy." Dion says that a messenger summoned the patricians by name, but that the people were convened by the blowing of a horn.[3] But the splendid military government which soon grew up, gave both state employment and riches to that class once distinguished for their industry and frugality. Agriculture was abandoned to slaves, and men branded for crimes: it was no longer deemed an honourable employment. Luxury and habits of profusion made it necessary for conspicuous men to acquire the means of indulging in them, at the expense of principle and patriotism. At length when sensual gratifications became dearer to a majority of the Romans than liberty, the republic was overthrown, and military despotism accomplished the circle of military influence; extinguished every spark of light and liberty; stripped the empire of its moral and physical power, and left it unmindful of its past glorious existence, to perish in a blind and helpless old age.

Marcus Tullius Cicero was born at Arpinum, a city of the Samnites, which had long enjoyed the freedom of Rome. His family was an ancient one, and of the equestrian order; which comprehended the most respectable gentry of the empire, who were only inferior in rank to the patricians. Having assumed the manly gown at his sixteenth year, he immediately began to acquire a knowledge of the laws of his country, under the two Scævolas, eminent persons of that day. The Marsian war, and the civil broils of Marius and Sylla, the former of whom was also a native of Arpinum, occurred during the prosecution of his civil studies; and although they gave some interruption to them, yet these violent contentions falling immediately under his observation, he became at an early period accustomed to consider the political situation of his country. These circumstances no doubt had some influence in deciding his future career; although the rare natural activity of his mind would perhaps have led him under any situation to the investigation of all moral and physical relations. 14Prompted by this impulse, he now began the study of Grecian philosophy under the learned Athenians who fled to Rome from the persecutions of Mithridates, and afterwards perfected himself in it under Molo the Rhodian; a man so distinguished, that he was permitted to address the Roman Senate in the Greek tongue without an interpreter. About the age of twenty-six, with his mind filled with all the knowledge taught at that period, he first began to plead at the Forum. His celebrated successful defence of S. Roscius was made soon after, in which he braved, what the other Roman orators had not dared to do, the resentment of Sylla. By this bold measure, the generosity of his character, as well as the force of his talents, were developed, and his reputation established as the most powerful orator of Rome. He visited Athens not long after this period, partly to avoid the displeasure of Sylla, and partly to renew the study of philosophy, which he here pursued with great ardour. His friend Atticus, who was at Athens at the same time, had embraced the Epicurean doctrines; but Cicero appears at this early period to have believed in a future state; a doctrine which at a later period he has most eloquently recorded in his celebrated Dream of Scipio. At the end of two years, he returned to Rome, greatly improved by his intercourse with the philosophers and orators of Greece and Asia.

15In his thirty-first year, and not long after his marriage, he was elected to the quæstorship, which opened his way to the Senate. One of the provinces of Sicily fell to him by lot, and he exercised his quæstorial functions with such moderation and ability, as to induce the Sicilians to confer extraordinary honours upon him at the termination of his year; when he returned to Rome, determined henceforward to withdraw himself as little as possible from the eyes of the Roman people. In his thirty-seventh year he received the unanimous suffrages of all the tribes for the edileship, which introduced him into the magistracy. The exhibition of the shows and games, which was the province of the ediles, was conducted by Cicero with great satisfaction to the people, and without injuring materially his own private fortune. In this he achieved a difficult point, which marks his great prudence and address. So great had the affection of the people now become for him, that at three different elections for prætor, he was each time placed at the head of the list by the unanimous vote of all the centuries. In his forty-third year, having been very diligent in strengthening his interest, he became a candidate for the consulship with others; among whom were L. Sergius Cataline: but such was his popularity that he was saluted consul by acclamation of the people before the votes were counted. He received also a 16strong support from the patricians, who had uniformly been opposed to his advancement; but Cicero's reputation for knowledge and probity was so great, and the times were becoming so critical, that they deemed the government safe in his hands. The patricians at this time were of the faction of Sylla, to which also Cataline belonged: and the Tribunes and the people were of the Marian faction; at the head of which was Julius Cæsar, a near relation to Marius. Although Cæsar, and Cicero were both on the popular side, yet they were not united upon any common principles of order. Cæsar was always individually opposed to him: and when Cicero being consul, was endeavouring in the senate to bring the associates of Cataline to punishment; Cæsar defended them, and even indirectly encouraged their cause, by declaring his disbelief in the immortality of the soul. The suppression of this conspiracy of Cataline, Cethegus, Lentulus and many others, among whom Cæsar was generally numbered, raised the reputation of Cicero to the greatest height. By his incessant vigilance, Rome was saved from the horrors of a general massacre and pillage. The greatest honours were paid him by the senate and equestrian order: and for the first time the sublime epithet of "Father of his Country" was addressed to a Roman citizen in the 17senate, in the person of Cicero.[4] This great action of his life he most feelingly alludes to in the introduction to his first book of the Republic. "Nor is my name forgotten," &c. The feelings too which the circumstances attending the very last act of his consulship excited in him, are eloquently pourtrayed in a passage immediately following. It was the custom for the consul at the expiration of his office, to make a speech in the assembly of the people, and to swear that he had executed his duties with fidelity. When he was already in the rostra, and was about to address the whole people assembled on this interesting occasion; Metellus, a new tribune, prompted by the officious spirit of popular authority, which often delights to mortify the great and good, forbade the consul to address the people, alleging that Cicero having caused Lentulus and the rest to suffer death without being heard in their defence, did not deserve to be heard himself. Whereat with an enthusiastic presence of mind peculiar to himself, he swore with a loud voice that he had saved the republic: and the multitude moved by a generous feeling which the demagogues had no time to tamper with, more than atoned to him for the intended affront from their tribune, by a simultaneous shout that he had sworn 18nothing but the truth,[5] and by accompanying him from the Forum to his own house.

In this most glorious year of his life, and at the very time when he was occupied in saving his country, Octavius Cæsar was born; by whose arts and influence Cicero, as well as the republic, were not more than twenty years after destroyed. And although he had acted so noble a part toward his country, which under his government had been saved from the most profligate attempt that had yet been made upon its liberties; and enjoyed the highest rank in the senate, and the first consideration from all good men; corruption had now reached such a height, that pre-eminence in virtue, shining forth in so active a citizen as Cicero, who was constantly thwarting the designs of bad men, served but to unite their efforts against him. He became henceforward the object of their hatred and vengeance. Cæsar, who did not believe in a future state, and who consequently had no principle to restrain him, was constantly plotting means to usurp the government. Pompey, in whose interest Cicero had always been, and who at the close of the Mithridatic war had become the most powerful man in the Republic, was afraid to disoblige the numerous enemies of Cicero, and declined even to 19strengthen him by a public approbation of the measures he had taken to suppress the conspiracy of Catiline. The luxurious and the corrupt, who far outnumbered the rest, were willing to sell the republic and themselves to the highest bidders. The people were as usual the tools of demagogues. Every thing conspired to accelerate the downfall of the republic. In the face of these fearful odds stood Cicero, a large majority of the senate, and of the equestrian order, which comprehended the independent landholders and gentry of the Roman nation: and with but little other support than the satisfaction of being engaged in the noblest of causes, the maintenance of regular government. It is most painful to look back upon the history of the degradation of such a people; corrupted and ruined by their blind admiration of that falsest of all idols, military glory.

An event occurred the year after his consulate, which brought him into a new conflict with some of the worst of these men. P. Clodius, at this time a quæstor, a vicious and debauched young man of family, and who possessed many personal advantages, had an intrigue with Cæsar's wife Pompeia. Satiated with ordinary voluptuousness, he disguised himself as a woman, and entered the house of Pompeia in the night time, when she with

5

other distinguished Roman matrons, was celebrating the mysteries of the Bona Dea, or Patroness of Chastity. He was discovered and fled. Such was the respect in which these mysteries, at which women alone officiated, were held, that the profanation excited the utmost indignation throughout the city. Even Cæsar found it necessary to put away his wife. The senate directed the consuls to prepare a law for the trial of Clodius before the people, which was resisted by one of the tribunes friendly to Clodius. At length it was agreed that a law should be passed to try him before the prætor and a select number of judges. Clodius rested his defence upon an alibi, which he endeavoured to sustain by witnesses. When Cicero was called to give his deposition, he was insulted by the mob which adhered to Clodius; but such was the veneration in which he was held, that the judges stood up, and received him with great honour. He testified that Clodius had been with him in his house in Rome on the very day of the pollution. Cæsar who was also called, said that he was ignorant of the whole affair; although it occurred in his own house, and in the presence of his mother and sister, who had deposed to the truth of the accusation. Being asked, why then he had put away his wife? he answered, "Because those who are connected with me, must be as free from suspicion as from crime."[6]

That the wife of Cæsar must be free even from suspicion, is a saying that has passed down to our days: yet too many who have heard it are ignorant of the circumstances attending its origin. We read the commentaries of Cæsar at school, and are fired with admiration at his talents and successes. We are thus prepared to pity his death and the manner of it. But the military and political glories of Cæsar, can never furnish an apology for a profligate private life; and a memorable saying is stripped of every attraction, when we know that it was uttered by the lips of a perjured atheist.

In a letter to Atticus, Cicero draws a curious picture of the judges selected to try this famous cause; a majority of whom appears to have been packed from the outcasts of all the orders, and to have been paid for the occasion. Clodius was acquitted by a majority of thirty-one voices over twenty-five. Upon their appointment some of them had requested a guard from the senate to protect them from the mob. Upon which occasion, Catulus a distinguished member of the senate, very facetiously asked one of the judges, "why they wanted a guard, and whether it was to protect the money which Clodius had bribed them with?"

After his acquittal, Clodius was wont to attempt to throw ridicule upon Cicero in the senate, finding it vain to encounter him in argument, and hoping to divert in some degree the force of his attacks. "So the judges" said Clodius, "would give no credit to your oath." "Twenty-five of them did," replied Cicero: "the rest would give you none it seems, but made you pay beforehand."

After the return of Pompey to Rome, as well as of Cæsar from Spain, a triumvirate of interests was formed between these two and Crassus: each having his own ascendancy in view. Cæsar, to make the interest it was thus intended to direct against the independence of the republic, still stronger, made overtures to Cicero, who declined connecting himself with them. At length Cæsar openly declared against him, and favoured the election of Clodius to the tribunate, in the which he succeeded. Being now in authority, he brought forward the law, that whoever had taken away the life of a Roman citizen, uncondemned, should be interdicted bread and water. This was directed against Cicero, in relation to his consular acts respecting the conspirators; and affected him so much, that although the law was in general terms, and his name was not mentioned in it, he changed his garments, and appeared abroad sordidly dressed to attract the compassion of the people. The young Romans of liberal character, to the number of twenty thousand also changed their dress, and accompanied him; soliciting the favour of all in authority, and of the people, against the passage of this law. But the combination of bad men proved too strong against him, and Pompey having refused his protection, Cicero was induced by the advice of his friends, to withdraw himself into a temporary exile from Rome. This humiliating event took place in his forty-ninth year. During his absence his residences both in town and country, which were upon a scale commensurate with his dignity, were despoiled; and together with the furniture appropriated by the consuls and by Clodius. At length the daring insolence of that tribune, and the perpetual broils he occasioned, began to indispose all men against him, except his immediate profligate retainers. Advantage was taken of this to propose in the senate the recall of Cicero; which finally prevailed at a very numerous convocation of the senators and magistrates; Clodius alone giving a dissenting voice. At its final passage into a law by the Roman people, the field of Mars was crowded with their assembled centuries. Such was the public veneration for him, that voters from every town in Italy were present to insure the passage of a law which restored so great a benefactor to his country. All the centuries concurred in an act thus most solemnly passed by the whole Roman people. In anticipation of the event, he left Dyrrhachium in Macedonia, and soon after his arrival at Brundisium, where his daughter Tullia had come to meet him, he received the welcome news from Rome. His journey was a continued triumph, and he was received on his arrival at the city in the most enthusiastic manner. An insufficient sum of money was voted to him to rebuild his mansions. When he had almost finished his palatine house, it was attacked by one of Clodius' mobs, and destroyed. Broils and slaughters were now so common in the streets of Rome, that gladiators were retained to assist in these feuds; in which the consuls of the same year were sometimes opposed to each other. Cicero who had now reached his fifty-first year, was again made to feel how unremitting is the hatred of enemies, and uncertain the support of friends. Public virtue appeared to him to have no longer any value in the eyes of the Romans. He saw that every man attended more to his private safety and advancement, than to the public peace and dignity of the city; and perceiving the necessity of a powerful protector for himself and family in his old age, he appears from one of his letters to have determined to conform himself in every thing to the pleasure of Pompey. We also see him from time to time engaged in agreeable services to Cæsar, with whom Pompey was yet connected. Experience and persecution appear to have induced him to adopt a course foreign to the character of the perfect citizen he has pourtrayed in his republic. In his fourth epistle to Atticus, he says[7] "If they will not be friendly to me who possess no power, I must endeavour to make those like me who have the power of being useful. 'I told you so long ago,' you will say; I know that you did, and I was an ass for not taking your advice." The opinion too of his friend Cælius, would have great weight with most men, in such disturbed times. "It cannot have escaped you, that the duty of men amidst domestic dissensions, is to espouse the honestest side, as long as the contention is of a civil nature, and force is not used. But when it comes to wars and camps, they should take the strongest side, and consider that the best which is the most safe."[8]

The influence of Cæsar was now becoming very conspicuous. His military career in Gaul, his generosity, and the universality of his talents, gave him at length a pre-eminence over Pompey in the public estimation. Pompey and Crassus had entered into the consulship with little observance of constitutional forms; and, with as little deference to the senate, had caused provinces to be assigned to them for five years. Spain and Africa to Pompey. Syria and the fatal Parthian 26war to Crassus. This triumvirate had now almost the whole Roman military force at their command.

It was in the spring of the next year, that Cicero at his Cuman villa, began his famous work on government. He was now advancing into his fifty-fourth year, and it appears that he had completed his work before he entered upon his command in Cilicia. His military career was distinguished by great activity and judgment. He was saluted emperor by the army upon one of his military successes, and returned gladly to Rome at the end of the year. During the remainder of his eventful life, he appears to have found comfort only in the cultivation of philosophy and letters. The corruption of the Romans, the ruin of the republic, the death of his beloved daughter, and his separation from the wife he had lived with thirty years, embittered his days. He was too conspicuous a man not to be affected by all the political changes which took place. Crassus perished in the Parthian war; and Cæsar, as soon as he felt himself strong enough, crossed the Rubicon, which was the limit of his military command, and marched upon Rome, from which Pompey and the senate ingloriously fled. Cicero at length felt himself also constrained to follow the fortunes of Pompey, because he believed the dignity of the Roman name was alone to be found under his banners. And when the battle of Pharsalia left Cæsar 27sole master of the Roman world, he submitted to Cæsar, because there was no other government to submit to. But he rejoiced in his death, of which he was a spectator, and to the last, gave all the aid in his power to the patriots who sought to raise the liberties of his country. In his latter days, he showed an invincible spirit, defying the profligate Anthony in the plenitude of his power. And when the assassins of the second and more bloody triumvirate surprised him, he ordered his servants to set down the litter in which they were carrying him, and forbade them to defend him. Then undauntedly stretching out his neck, he bade his executioners do their pleasure; happy to escape from so much misery, to the immortality he had always believed in. This occurred when he was just entering his sixty-fourth-year.

This rapid sketch of the transactions of Cicero's times, will, it is hoped, not be deemed impertinent, but may rather be considered as assisting the general reader to form an adequate estimate of the great object which Cicero had in view, when he drew up this celebrated treatise, which was to revive the veneration of the Roman people for their ancient institutions, now in danger from the machinations of lawless men, at the head of whom was Cæsar, who denying in the senate a future existence, expressed his contempt for all religion. But 28it has been objected to Cicero that he was insincere, and that he called upon his countrymen to venerate what was often the object of his ridicule. The leading men of Rome who formed the sacerdotal order, from the earliest periods and under all circumstances maintained their influence over the people, chiefly by that religion they had been brought up in the veneration of, and especially by the observance of auspices. But in time the credulity of the Romans began to relax. Men like Cicero had for their religion the glorious doctrine of the immortality of the soul, and a great majority of his enlightened equals no doubt entertained his opinions. Others, and among them was his brother Quintus, from various motives, as has always been the case in the history of superstitions, persevered in the prejudices they had received from education. Prejudices acquired in infancy from our earliest and dearest protectors, and to relinquish which, seems to require the relinquishment of all reverence for those we most venerate. When therefore Cicero ridicules the religious observances of his times, it is to enlightened men he sometimes addresses himself; just as men have in all times laughed at absurdities they do not care publicly to assail: and at other times he may have used his ridicule to expose the most stupid superstitions indiscriminately to all. When in his Republic he praises the institution of auspices, however he may be charged with inconsistency, it was done from great and public motives, and not from selfish ones. There is no hypocrisy in this conduct, as we understand the word; and if we examine the whole bearing of Cicero's life, the policy which the circumstances of it, sometimes obliged him to, will not offend liberal minds. In estimating therefore the character of Cicero, it is well to remember Dr. Middleton's remark in his preface "and in every thing especially that relates to Cicero, I would recommend the reader to contemplate the whole character, before he thinks himself qualified to judge of its separate parts, on which the whole will always be found the surest comment."

The first book is the most complete of the whole six: the opening however is imperfect. Cicero in his own person enters into a discussion whether governments should be administered by contemplative philosophers, or by active practical men. He recapitulates the arguments on both sides of the question, often discussed by the ancients, and decides the question in consonance with those feelings which had governed his very active life. The eloquence and force of some of the passages are inimitable. They will be applicable to all times as long as civil government exists among men. But in this country where the experiment of a popular government is trying upon so comprehensive a scale, the grandeur of the sentiments deserves the attention of every man. As where he states as an argument of those who shun active occupations, that it is dangerous to meddle with public affairs in turbulent times, and disgraceful to associate with the low and disreputable men who are conspicuous at those periods; that it is vain to hope to restrain the mad violence of the vulgar, or to withdraw from such a contest without injury; "As if," he adds with a generous enthusiasm, "there could be a more just cause for good and firm men, endowed with noble minds, to stand forth in aid of their country, than that they may not be subject to bad men; nor suffer the republic to be lacerated by them, before the desire of saving it may come too late."

After disposing of this question, he proceeds with great address to open the plan of his work, and presents in all the beautiful simplicity of the times, Scipio, his friend Lælius, with some of their most accomplished cotemporaries, seated, not in the gorgeous saloon of a Lucullus or Crassus, but in the sunny part, because it was the winter season, of the lawn of Scipio's country place; where they had convened to pass the Latin holidays in discussing philosophical questions. Here, upon an inquiry being instituted into the cause of two suns reported to have been seen in the heavens, occasion is found to introduce in a very pleasing manner, the astronomical knowledge of the day, which Cicero was well versed in. Scipio is made here to deliver a magnificent passage, beginning at the 17th section. "Who can perceive any grandeur in human affairs," &c.[9] This inquiry about celestial phenomena, which appeared so foreign to a philosophical investigation on the principles of government, is admirably closed and without the abruptness being perceived, by Lælius asking how it can interest him that Scipio should be solicitous about the two suns, "when he does not inquire the cause why two senates, and almost two people exist in one republic." At the general request Scipio consents to deliver his opinion of government. He defines a republic to be the "public thing," or common interest of all: and he shews most satisfactorily that human beings congregate not on account of their weakness, but that they are led thereto by the social principle, which is innate in man, and leads him even in the midst of the greatest abundance to seek his fellow. He successively examines the despotic, the aristocratic, and democratic forms of government: their advantages and disadvantages; and concludes that a fourth kind of government, moderated and compounded from those three is most to 32be approved. This is subsequently recurred to and enlarged upon. Many persons will be surprised that the balanced representative form of government, which has but in modern times received the sanction of the wisest nations, should have been shadowed forth in an apparently speculative opinion, two thousand years ago. We must however remember, that in the numerous small independent states of Greece; their various forms of government, the tyranny of their kings, the oppression of the aristocracies, and the violence of the people, had produced many discussions among their writers. Few of these have come down to us. Yet Cicero was familiar with them, and it is evident that his plan of a mixed government was drawn from this source. There is a passage to this effect preserved in the Anthology of Stobæus, of Hyppodamus. He says that royalty, which is a copy of divinity, is insufficient, on account of the degeneracy of human nature. That it must be limited by an aristocracy, where the principle of emulation leads men to excel each other: and that the citizen also should be admitted into that mixed government as of right: but cautiously, as the people are apt to fall into disorders. These opinions also flattered the Romans, for in fact it was substantially their own form of government, which consisted of consuls, patricians, and the people and their tribunes.

33Scipio in the 43d section, gives an eloquent passage from Plato, where the excesses of the multitude are painted in the strongest language; a passage which might well have been inspired by the French revolution.

Scipio opens the second book with the origin of the Roman people, adopting the received opinions concerning the early history of Rome, of Romulus, and the succeeding kings. These opinions have of late, been much controverted. Niebuhr whose erudition appears to be inimitable, whatever success he may be thought to have had in shaking them, has substituted nothing satisfactory in their place, at least as far as we may gather from his first volume. One thing may be safely asserted, that Cicero might well present in his republic, those traditions of the times, as the real history of his country, because the Roman people were acquainted with no other. He could not call upon them to venerate the founders of Rome and their institutions, and tell them at the same time they had never existed. Niebuhr himself strengthens the account given at section 19, Book II., of the Greek descent of the first Tarquin, by observing that the clay vases made at Tarquinii were painted, and resembled in colour and drawing some discovered near Corinth. He says they are found only in the district of Tarquinii, and 34that the circumstance implies a peculiar intercourse between Corinth and Tarquinii.

In the 22d section of the 2d Book, is another passage with which Niebuhr is not satisfied, and which even Professor Mai terms "vexatissimum locum." Cicero says the Roman people were distributed by Servius into six classes, whose entire elective force was one hundred and ninety-three centuries. To give the landed proprietors who were rated in the first class, a majority of this number, or ninety-seven votes, three centuries of horse with six suffrages, meaning those inscribed in the great census or register, in contradistinction to the horsemen set apart from the mass of the whole people; the century of carpenters, and the first class, constituted together eighty-nine centuries. Eight more centuries taken from the other five classes and added to this number, made ninety-seven, being a majority of one over ninety-six, and thus in Cicero's words "Confecta est vis, populi universa." The unwearied erudition of Niebuhr, to which great deference is due, is not satisfied with the simplicity of this statement of the Roman Constitution, but assails it with an unusual bitterness of critical spirit. He supposes the passage from its genuine state to have been corrupted by successive transcribers and commentators, to the order in which Professor Mai has thought proper to 35give it to the public, and that in its original state it stood thus. "Nunc rationem videtis esse talem ut prima classis, addita centuria quæ ad summum usum urbis fabris tignariis est data: LXXXI centurias habeat; quibus ex CXIV centuriis, tot enim reliquæ sunt, equitum centuriæ cum sex suffragiis solæ si accesserunt," &c.

"Now you will perceive the plan was such, that the first class, a century being added from the carpenters on account of their great utility to the city, consisted of eighty-one centuries; to which if from the one hundred and fourteen centuries, for so many remain, only the centuries of horse with six suffrages are added," &c. I forbear to add his very curious reasons for this proposed restoration, and which, not to be deemed extravagant, require to be judged by those familiar with the emendations of ancient MSS. It will be perceived, however, that he makes the whole number of centuries to consist of one hundred and ninety-five; and that he gives the landed proprietors a majority of ninety-nine over the ninety-six centuries belonging to the other five classes, which appears superfluous in a system which aimed at the appearance of moderation, "ne superbum esset." Substantially the system appears to have been this. The Roman people were distributed into six classes, having one hundred and ninety-three centuries 36or votes. The first class consisting of men of rank and property, with the centuries of horse, had ninety-six votes; leaving ninety-seven votes to the other five classes. In order, however, to give the ascendancy to the first class in the least offensive way, the century of blacksmiths and carpenters was added to the first class, under pretence of their great utility to the city; but really because they were dependent upon the first class and the cavalry for employment, and could be relied upon. In this manner the first class secured a majority of ninety-seven votes. The second book closes with a declaration from Scipio, that unless the most perfect justice is observed, no government can prosper.

The third book opens with a philosophical analysis of the faculties of man, introductory to the great principle of the immutable nature of justice, which it appears was fully discussed in this book, of which so small a portion is preserved. A splendid picture is drawn in the second section of an accomplished statesman, such as Cicero himself had aimed to be, and which from a passage in one of his letters to Atticus, appears to have been farther elaborated in the sixth book. It relates to a triumph about which he felt some anxiety after his government of Cilicia. "If this idea of a triumph which even you approve, had not been infused into me, you would not have had to look far for 37the perfect citizen described in the sixth book."[10] Philus is called upon to defend the cause of injustice after the manner of Carneades the Greek sophist. The powerful passage contained in the seventeenth section is delivered by him. It was reserved for Lælius to close the discussion as the advocate of justice. Scarce any part of his discourse is preserved. Some fragments have, however, been collected by Professor Mai, preserved by Nonius the Philologist, and by Lactantius. In the one, Lælius is made to declare, that the Roman youth ought not to be permitted to listen to Carneades, who if he thought as he spoke, was a bad man; and if he was not, as he preferred to believe, his discourse was nevertheless detestable. One of the passages from Lanctantius is that well known exposition of eternal right, or natural law of justice of which conscience is the voice.

"There is indeed a law, right reason, which is in accordance with nature; existing in all, unchangeable, eternal. Commanding us to do what is right, forbidding us to do what is wrong. It has dominion over good men, but possesses no influence over bad ones. No other law can be substituted for it, no part of it can be taken away, nor can it be abrogated altogether. Neither the people or the senate can absolve us from 38it. It wants no commentator or interpreter. It is not one thing at Rome, and another thing at Athens: one thing to-day, and another thing to-morrow; but it is a law eternal and immutable for all nations and for all time. God, the sole Ruler, and universal Lord, has framed and proclaimed this law. He who does not obey it, renounces himself, and is false to his own nature: he brings upon himself the direst tortures, even when he escapes human punishments."[11]

The fourth book of which a mere fragment is preserved, appears to have treated of domestic manners, the education of youth, and of Roman life, public and private. We have lost here many fine pictures of the simplicity of Roman manners, at that flourishing period of the republic, as well as of the progress of luxury, which was not inconsiderable. A fragment of this book is preserved in Nonius, where Scipio opposes the collection of a revenue, necessary perhaps to make good those deficiencies which extravagance had produced. "Nolo enim eundem populum imperatorem et portitorem esse terrarum. Optimum autem et in privatis familiis et in republica vectigal duco esse parsimoniam." "I am not willing that the same people should be the sovereigns and the toll-gatherers of the world. 39I look upon economy to be the best revenue for the republic, and for private individuals."

The fifth book is also a mere fragment. St. Augustin has preserved some notices of it, from which it appears that it treated very much of the ancient Roman institutions, with a view to show the degeneracy of the times in which Cicero wrote. In the fifth section of this book, he speaks of the comfortable enjoyment of life depending upon legal marriages and lawful children; from whence perhaps we may gather the obligation which the dissolute manners of the times had laid him under, of asserting the value of these ties, as well as his own veneration for them.

Of the sixth book no part whatever has come down to us with this MSS: but the important fragment on a future state preserved in Macrobius, warrants our supposing that he was naturally led in a treatise so highly philosophical, to pass from the consideration of human morals, to the great object which moral conduct has in view: the resisting of human weakness, for the sake of fitting the immortal part of our nature for a higher condition of being. The dream of Scipio, encumbered as it is by some of the pedantry of the schools, is a production of the highest order, upon this most sublime of all subjects.

1. 40His. Nat. 18. 3. 1.

2. Cato de Re Rustica. Majores enim nostri, &c.

3. Dio. 11. 8. Gellius xv. 27.

4. Roma patrem patriæ Ciceronem libera dixit. Juv. 8.

5. Magna Voce me vere jurasse juravit. Ep. fam. 5. 2.

6. Quoniam, inquit, meos tam suspicione quam crimine judico carere oportere. Suet. J. Cæs. 74.

7. Sed quoniam qui nihil possunt, &c.

8. Ep. fam. 8. 14.

9. "Quid porro aut præclarum putet in rebus humanis." Lib. 1. xvii.

10. Let. to Att. vii. 3.

11. Lact. Inst. vi. 8.

CICERO'S REPUBLIC.

BOOK I.

I. For without the strong feeling of patriotism, neither had G. Duelius, Aulus Atilius or L. Metellus freed us from the terror of Carthage; or the two Scipios extinguished with their blood the rising flame of the second punic war. Quintus Maximus would not have weakened, nor M. Marcellus have crushed the one which was springing up with still greater strength: or P. Africanus turning it from the gates of this city, have borne it amid the walls of our enemies. Yet it was not thought unbecoming in M. Cato, an unknown and a new man, by whom all of us who emulate his course are led as a bright example of industry and virtue, to enjoy the repose of Tusculum, that healthy and convenient situation. That insane man, however, as some have considered him, preferred when urged by no necessity, to contend amid those waves and tempests to extreme old age; rather than pass his days in the most agreeable manner, amid so much ease and tranquillity. Men without number I omit, each of whom were benefactors to the State, and who are not far removed from the remembrance of this generation. I forbear to commemorate them, lest any one should reproach me with neglecting to speak of himself or his immediate friends. This one truth I would mark, that nature has so strongly implanted in man the necessity of virtue, and so powerful an inclination to defend the common welfare, that this principle overcomes all the blandishments of voluptuousness and ease.

II. Yet to possess virtue, like some art, without exercising it, is insufficient. Art indeed, when not effective, is still comprehended in science. The efficacy of all virtue consists in its use. Its greatest end is the government of states, and the perfection not in words but in deeds, of those very things which are taught in the halls. For nothing is propounded by philosophers, concerning what is esteemed to be just and proper, that is not confirmed and assured by those who have legislated for states. For from whence springs piety, or from whom religion? Whence the law, either of nations, or that which is called civil? Whence justice, faith, equity? Whence modesty, continence, the dread of turpitude, the love of praise and esteem? Whence fortitude in trouble and dangers? From those who having laid a foundation for these things in early education, have strengthened some of them by the influence of manners, and sanctioned others by the influence of laws. Of

Xenocrates, one of the noblest of philosophers, it is said, that when he was asked what his disciples learnt of him, he replied "to do that of their own choice, which the laws enjoined them to do," therefore the citizen who obliges every one by the authority and fear of the law to do that, which philosophers by reasoning, 43with difficulty persuade a few to do, is to be preferred to those learned men who only dispute about these things. For which of their orations, however exquisite, can be compared in value to a well constituted state, to public right and to morals. Truly as great and powerful cities, as Ennius says, are as I think, to be preferred to villages and castles; so those who stand pre-eminent in those cities, in authority and counsel, are to be esteemed far before those in wisdom, who are altogether ignorant of the conduct of public affairs. And since we are chiefly urged by a desire to increase the possessions of the human race, and seek by our counsels and labours, to surround the life of man with gratification and security, and are incited by the instincts of nature to these enjoyments; let us hold the course which was always that of the best men: nor attend to those signals which speculative philosophers make from their retirement, to allure back those who are already far advanced.

III. Against these reasons so certain and so clear, it is urged by those who are opposed to us: first, the labour to be undergone in preserving the public welfare; a slight impediment to the zealous and industrious, not alone in matters of such high import, but in inferior things: whether in studies or in official stations; and to be despised even in affairs of business. To this they add the dangers to which life is exposed, and the dread of death, which brave men scorn; being wont to view it as more wretched to waste away by infirmity and old age, than to seize an occasion to devote that life to the advantage of their country, which one day must be rendered 44to nature. It is here however they deem themselves most successful and eloquent, when they bring forward the calamities of eminent men, and the injuries heaped upon them by their ungrateful countrymen. Here come the instances in Grecian history. Miltiades, the conqueror and subduer of the Persians, with those wounds yet streaming, which he received in front, in the height of victory: preserved from the weapons of the enemy, to waste away his life in the chains of his countrymen. And Themistocles proscribed and driven from the country he had freed, flying, not to the harbours of that Greece he had preserved, but to the barbarous shores he had harrassed. Nor indeed are instances wanting among the Athenians of levity and cruelty towards great numbers of their citizens; instances which springing up repeatedly among them, are said also to have abounded too conspicuously in our city. For either the exile of Camillus, the misfortune of Ahala, the ill will towards Nasica, or the expulsion of Lenas, or the condemnation of Opimus is remembered: or the flight of Metellus, the sad overthrow of C. Marius, the cutting off of the most eminent citizens, or the destruction of many of them, which soon after followed. Nor indeed is my name forgotten. And I judge that deeming themselves to owe both life and ease to my peril and counsel, they have a more deep and tender remembrance of me. But it is not easy to explain how they who cross the seas for the sake of observing or describing * * *

[Two pages wanting.]
45IV. * * * * At the expiration of my consulship, when in the assembly of the Roman people, I swore that the republic had been saved by my exertions, which they confirmed by universal acclamation, I was requited for the cares and vexations of every injury. Albeit my reverses had more honour than pain attached to them, and less disquietude than glory. Greater was my pleasure at receiving the approbation of good men, than my regret at observing the satisfaction of the bad. But had it happened otherwise, as I said, what

complaint could I make? Nothing unforeseen could have occurred, nor more grievous than I might have expected for so many of my deeds. For I was one who could well have gathered greater fruits from ease than others, on account of the agreeable variety of the studies I had pursued from my childhood; and if any disaster had overtaken the republic, I need not have sustained a greater share of it, but have divided it equally with the rest. I hesitated not to oppose myself to those stormy tempests, and almost raging waves, for the sake of preserving my fellow citizens, and of accomplishing at my own risk the common safety of all. For our country has not produced us, or educated us under a law, that she is entitled to no support on our part, lending herself as it were to our convenience only; furnishing a secure refuge, and a tranquil and peaceful asylum to our indolence: but rather holds as pledges to her, to be employed for her benefit, the many and great faculties of our mind, genius, and reason; and only permits us to appropriate to our private purposes, that portion of them, of which she stands in no need.

46V. The pretences which are urged for the enjoyment of indolence are not to be listened to. As when it is stated that the public affairs are meddled with by men worthy of no confidence, with whom it is disgraceful to associate: yet to contend against whom is a miserable and dangerous effort, especially when the multitude is excited. For which reason a prudent man ought not to take the reins, when he is not able to restrain the mad and untameable violence of the vulgar: or a generous man expose himself to the lashes of contumely in a strife with low and outrageous adversaries: or a wise man hope to withdraw from such a contest without injury. As if there could well be a more just cause for good and firm men, endowed with noble minds, to stand forth in aid of their country, than that they may not be subject to bad men; nor suffer the republic to be lacerated by them, before the desire of saving it may come too late.

VI. But who can approve of their exception, that a wise man ought not to take upon him any part of the public affairs, unless an occasion of extraordinary need should drive him to it? as if indeed a greater necessity could ever have happened to any one, than occurred to myself. How could I have been useful then, had I not been consul? and how could I have been consul, had I not pursued that course of life from my youth, which belonging to the equestrian rank, in which I was born, enabled me to attain the first honours of the state? No man therefore can assume at pleasure the ability of aiding in the public service, however urgent the danger may be, unless he stands in that relation 47to his country, which fits him for the occasion. And it appears to me most marvellous, that in the discourse of learned men, they who declare themselves unable to steer in a calm sea, because they have never been taught, nor have ever studied the subject, talk of taking the helm in the midst of the greatest storms. For these very men openly declare, and pride themselves greatly upon it, that they have never studied or taught the mode of establishing or protecting the public interest; which they think the exclusive province, not of learned and erudite men, but of those who are practised in these matters. What consistency is there then in promising to aid the republic in times of peril, when they are incapable of the easier task of directing it in the calmest moments? And although, in truth, the philosopher is not wont of his own accord, to consider the details of state affairs, unless called upon by the times to do it, when indeed he will not decline what duty imposes on him; nevertheless, I judge the knowledge of state affairs is least to be neglected by a wise man; that every thing may be familiar to him, for he cannot tell the moment, when it may be necessary for him to avail himself of his knowledge.

VII. These things I have somewhat enlarged upon, because the discussion proposed and undertaken by me in this work, was on government: and in order to prevent its being without effect, it was necessary in the first instance, to remove every doubt as to the duty of engaging in the public service. Nevertheless if there are any who are governed by the opinions of philosophers, let them turn their attention for a while, and listen 48to those who enjoy a proud pre-eminence among learned men, even when they have not borne any charge in the republic; still whom I deem from the extent of their studies, and their writings on government, to have been invested with functions appertaining to the public interest. But those seven, whom the Greeks call wise, I perceive have almost all been greatly engaged in public affairs. For there is no one thing in which human worth is more nearly allied to the power of the gods, than to found new states, or to preserve those already founded.

VIII. Concerning which matters, since it hath happened to me, to be deemed something worthy of memory in my administration of public affairs, and to possess some talent for unfolding them; not only in practice, but being versed too in the art of speaking and teaching: while of those before me, some were perfect in debate, yet unknown by their deeds; others of respectable parts for business, without the talent of oratory. Still it is not my intention here to bring forward any new system invented by myself, but to repeat a discussion, that took place at a certain period of our history, among our most illustrious and wise men, which was related to me a long time ago in my youth, by P. Rutilius Rufus, when we were at Smyrna together: in the which I think scarce any point was omitted that belongs to the consideration of these great matters.

IX. When P. Africanus, the son of Paulus, established Latin holidays in his gardens, during the consulate of Tuditanus, and Aquilius; and his most intimate friends had promised to visit him frequently at 49that season. On the morning of the first day, Q. Tubero, the eldest son of his sister, came. Pleased with his visit, and kindly addressing him "What! Tubero," said he, "is it you so early? I should have thought these holidays would have given you a favourable opportunity of pursuing your literary inquiries." "Why in truth," replied he, "I can apply all my leisure to my books, for they are always disengaged. But to find you at leisure, is very remarkable; especially at this time so critical for the republic." "So help me Hercules," said Scipio, "however you find me, it is more idle in appearance than in truth." "You must now," said Tubero, "relax your mind a little also, for several of us have determined if it is not inconvenient to you, to spend some of our leisure with you." "With all my heart," replied Scipio, "provided we may acquire some information thereby on philosophical subjects."

X. "Since you invite and encourage me to it yourself," said Tubero, "let us first converse, Africanus, before the others come, about the meaning of this double sun which has been spoken of in the senate. For those who declare that they have seen two suns, are neither few in number, nor insignificant persons: so that it appears to be of less importance to doubt the fact, than to inquire into the cause of it." "Would that we had with us our excellent Panætius," said Scipio, "who among other objects of knowledge, was so diligent an inquirer about celestial phenomena. As to myself, Tubero—for to you I will freely declare what I think; I am not drawn in to adopt in matters of this sort, the opinions of our friend, who pronounces things 50which are scarcely within the reach of conjecture, to be as manifest, as if he beheld them with his eyes, or could lay his hands upon them. On which account I am accustomed to consider Socrates much wiser, who leaves the consideration of such things aside, and teaches that the phenomena about which nature may be interrogated, are either beyond the force of human reason, or irrelevant to the conduct of human affairs." "I know not," rejoined Tubero, "what authority there is for the fact, that Socrates rejected all discussion upon such matters, and confined himself to the moral conduct of human life. For what author is to be commended, as more ample on that head than Plato; in whose writings, in many places, it is the custom of Socrates in discussing morals, the virtues, and finally public affairs; to allude studiously to the science of numbers, to geometry, and to harmony, after the Pythagorean mode." Scipio answered, "these things are as you say; but I dare say you have heard, Tubero, that Plato after the death of Socrates, was carried by the love of knowledge first into Egypt, afterwards into Italy and Sicily, that he might obtain an insight into the discoveries of Pythagoras. That he associated much with Archytas the Tarentine, and with Timæus of Locram. That he acquired the commentaries of Philolaus, and perceiving that the name of Pythagoras was at that time in great reputation in those places, he dedicated his time to the disciples of Pythagoras and to their opinions. But as he had loved Socrates alone, and wished to make all things conducive to his reputation, he interwove very skilfully the subtlety and humour of the Socratic style 51with the mysteries of Pythagoras, and with many branches of the arts."

As Scipio ceased to speak, he suddenly saw L. Furius approaching, and as soon as he had kindly saluted him, he took him by the hand, and placed him on his couch. And as P. Rutilius the accomplished preserver of this conversation appeared at the same time, saluting him also in the same manner, he bade him be seated near to Tubero. "What are you engaged in," said Furius; "hath our arrival broken in upon your conversation?" "Not in the least," replied Africanus, "for it is precisely about matters, such as Tubero has just been introducing, that thou art wont diligently to inquire into, and to investigate. And indeed our friend Rutilius was in the habit occasionally of discussing things of this kind with me, when we were under the walls of Numantia." "What is the subject you have fallen upon?" said Philus. "These two suns," replied he, "respecting which I am desirous of hearing your opinion."

XII. As he spoke this, a boy announced that Lælius was approaching, having already left his house; upon which Scipio having dressed himself, left his chamber, and had made but a few paces in the portico, when he saluted Lælius who was approaching, and those who were with him: Spurius Mummius, to whom he was particularly attached; Fannius, and Quintus Scævola, sons-in-law of Lælius, highly gifted young men of the quæstorial age. And having welcomed them all, he made another turn on the portico, placing Lælius in the middle; for in their friendship it was a 52sort of law between them, that Lælius did homage to Scipio as to a god, on account of his glorious pre-eminence in war; while in his turn Scipio, in private life, paid to Lælius all the reverence due to a parent, on account of his superior years. And having chatted a little together in various places, Scipio, who was very much enlivened and gratified with their arrival, was pleased to have them seated in a sunny place in a little meadow, on account of its being the winter season; which as they were about to do, M. Manilius came, a prudent and agreeable person, and very dear to them all; who being cordially saluted by Scipio and the rest, took his seat next to Lælius.

XIII. "It does not seem to me necessary," said Philus "that we should seek another subject of conversation on account of those who are arrived, but that we should observe more accuracy, and say something worthy of their ears." "What subject were you upon," said Lælius, "and what discussion are we come to be present at?" "Scipio was inquiring of me," replied Philus, "what my opinion was respecting the fact of two suns having been seen."

Lælius. "Why truly Philus, is there no longer any thing left for us to inquire about, touching our own domestic affairs, or those appertaining to the republic, that we must be exploring the things that are passing in the heavens?" "Dost thou then think," replied he, "that it does not concern our own mansions, to know what is passing, and what is done in that vast one, not the one surrounded by our walls, but that which constitutes the universe, and which the gods have given to us 53for a domicile, and a common country with themselves. Especially when if we are ignorant of them, many and very high matters will be hidden from us. As to myself, the contemplation and knowledge of these things delight me, as certainly as it does you, Lælius, and all who are eager in the pursuit of knowledge." "I offer no impediment," said Lælius, especially at this holiday time; but shall we hear any thing, or are we come too late?"

Philus. "Nothing has been discussed yet, and as the subject is entire, I freely concede to you, Lælius, the right of expressing your sentiments first."

Lælius. "Let us rather hear you, unless Manilius thinks, that some decree by way of compromise between these two suns may be adjusted; so that each may keep possession of its own part of the firmament." "You love still to banter that science, Lælius, in which I am proud to excel," replied Manilius, "and without which no one could know his own possession from anothers. But of that by and by. Let us now listen to Philus, who I perceive has a case of greater difficulty referred to him, than ever came before me or P. Mucius."

XIV. "I shall lay nothing new before you," said Philus, "nor any thing discovered or thought of by myself. I remember, however, that C. Sulpicius Gallus, a very learned man as you know; when this same phenomenon was stated to have been seen, being by chance in the house of M. Marcellus, who had been in the consulate with him; ordered a sphere to be placed before him, which the ancestor of M. Marcellus had taken from the conquered Syracusans, and brought out of 54their wealthy and embellished city; the only thing he had possessed himself of among so great a spoil. I had heard a great deal of this sphere, on account of the fame of Archimedes, but did not admire the construction of it so much; for another which Archimedes also had made, and which the same Marcellus had placed in the temple of virtue, was more elegant and remarkable in the general opinion. But subsequently, when Gallus began very scientifically to explain the nature of the mechanism; the Sicilian appeared to me to possess more genius, than human nature would seem to be capable of. Gallus said, that the other solid and full sphere was an old invention, and was first wrought by Thales of Miletas: but afterwards was delineated over with the fixed stars in the heavens by Eudoxus, the Cnidian, a disciple of Plato. The which adorned and embellished as it was by Eudoxus, Aratus who had no knowledge of astronomy, but a certain poetical faculty, many years afterwards extolled in his verses. The mechanism of this sphere, however, on which the motions of the sun, moon, and those five stars which are called wandering and irregular, are shown; could not be illustrated on that solid sphere. But what appeared very admirable in this invention of Archimedes was, that he had discovered a method of producing the unequal and various courses, with their dissimilar velocities, by one revolution. When Gallus put this sphere in motion, the moon was made to succeed the sun by as many revolutions of the brass circle, as it actually took days to do in the heavens. From which the same setting of the sun was produced on the sphere as in the heavens: and the moon fell on the very 55point, where it met the shadow of the earth, when the sun from the region * * * *

[About ten pages wanting.]
XV. * * * * * for he was a man I was very much attached to, and I know that my father Paulus esteemed and placed the highest value on him. I remember when I was but a boy, being with my father, who was then consul in Macedonia; that while we were encamped, our army was struck with a religious dread, because the full and splendid moon in the serenity of the night, was suddenly eclipsed. He being then our lieutenant, the year just before that in which he was declared consul, did not hesitate the following day, to pronounce openly in the camp, that it was no prodigy. And that what had then taken place, would always occur in future at those particular periods, when the position of the sun was such, that its rays could not fall upon the moon. "But how could he," asked Tubero, "make men half wild, comprehend such matters, or venture to speak of them before the unenlightened?"

Scipio. "Indeed he did, and with great * * * *

[About two pages wanting.]
* * * * * there was neither a haughty ostentation, nor any thing in his speech unbecoming a grave personage; and he accomplished a point of great importance, in removing from the disturbed minds of the men, the influence of an idle and fearful superstition.

XVI. There was an occurrence similar to this during the great war, which the Athenians and Lacedemonians waged against each other with so much inveteracy. 56Darkness being suddenly produced by the obscuration of the sun, and a prodigious fear taking possession of the minds of the Athenians. Pericles, the first man in the city, in authority, in eloquence, and in council; taught the citizens what he had himself learnt from Anaxagoras, whose pupil he had been: that it was an unavoidable appearance at the particular period, when the moon had placed herself immediately before the orb of the sun: and although it did not take place every lunar period; it could nevertheless be occasioned only by the moon's motion. Having convinced them by reasoning, he delivered the people from their apprehension. For it was then a strange and unknown reason to give for an eclipse, that the sun and moon were in opposition to each other, which it is said, was first observed by Thales the Milesian. At a later period, this had not escaped our Ennius, who wrote about the year 350 of the building of Rome, in the nones of June; that "the moon and night stood before the sun." So great, however, is the advancement of knowledge in these matters, that from this day, which we find noted in the principal annals, and by Ennius; the previous occultations of the sun are fixed up to that which took place in the reign of Romulus, in the nones of the fifth month. During which darkness, Romulus, whom the laws of nature indeed would have carried to the tomb, is said to have been borne by his virtue to heaven.

XVII. Then Tubero, "Dost thou not perceive Africanus, that what appeared otherwise to thee a while ago * * * * * *

[About two pages wanting.]

57* * * * * * "Who can perceive any grandeur in human affairs, whose eyes are accustomed to survey the empire of the gods? What are temporal things in the eyes of those conversant with eternal ones? What is there glorious to the contemplation of him, who looks at the small size of the earth; first as to its whole extent, then to that part of it which men inhabit? And yet we, confined to so small a portion of it, unknown to most nations, hope our name will be diffused to its utmost limits. What are lands, and houses, and flocks, and immense masses of gold and silver to him who neither considers them desirable nor calls them so: the fruition of which appears to him trifling, the use unsatisfactory, the possession uncertain: and which are often in the hands of the most contemptible of men? How fortunate may that man be esteemed, who alone claims a share in all things, not as the privilege of a citizen, but of a philosopher: not by civil rights, but by the common law of nature, which forbids any one to be the proprietor of aught, of the proper use of which he is ignorant! Who considers our consulships and high offices, not to be sought after for the sake of personal advantage or glory; not as things to be coveted, but to be undertaken as duties. The man finally who can say that of himself which my ancestor Africanus, as Cato writes, was wont to say, "that he never was more busy than when he was doing nothing; and that he never was less alone, than when nobody was with him."

For who can deem Dionysius to have accomplished a greater thing, when by the greatest exertion he snatched their liberties from the citizens, than Archimedes his 58countryman, who appearing to be occupied in nothing, produced this sphere of which we were but now conversing? Are they not more alone, who find no one in the forum or in the crowd who chooses to talk with them, than those who without any witness can converse with themselves; or as it were, be present at the councils of the most learned men, when they solace themselves with their discoveries and writings? Who in truth can imagine any one to be more rich, than the man who has no wants, beyond the simple calls of nature; or more powerful than him, who has attained the possession of al that he desires; or more blessed than him who is freed from all anxiety of mind? or what man's fortune is better established than his, who can carry along with him, or out of a shipwreck as men are wont to say, all his possessions? What command, what office, what kingdom can be preferred to that condition of mind, which looking down upon all things human, and esteeming them to be the objects of an inferior wisdom, turns ever to the contemplation of those things that are divine and eternal: persuaded that they only deserve to be called men, who are refined by the sciences of humanity? That which has been said of Plato, or of some other sage, appears to me therefore very excellent. Who being borne by a tempest to unknown lands, and cast on a desert shore, while his companions were apprehensive on account of their ignorance of the place, is said to have perceived geometrical figures described on the sand. Which when he saw, he bade them all be of good heart, for he had seen vestiges of men. Not that he judged so from the cultivation of the 59fields which he beheld, but from these indications of science. For all these reasons, Tubero, learning, and learned men, and these thy studies have always been pleasing to me.

XVIII. Then said Lælius, "I am not bold enough, Scipio, to speak of these things: nor even to thee, or Philus, or Manilius * * * * *

[Two pages wanting]
* * * * in his paternal house we have had a friend, worthy to be imitated by him.

"Ælius Sextus, conspicuously discreet and wise." That he was conspicuously discreet and wise, is said by Ennius, not because he sought after what he was not able to discover, but because he answered those who made inquiries of him, in a manner to solve their difficulties and anxieties, in whose mouth when arguing against the studies of Gallus, were always these words of Achilles, in Iphigenia.

"Astrology, its signs; how are they read in heaven?
When goat or scorpion, or ferocious names arise,
The obvious earth is shunned, to scrutinize the skies."

He also said, for many times and willingly I listened to him, that Zethus the author of Pacuvius, was too great an enemy to science. The Neoptolemus of Ennius pleased him more; who says that he likes to philosophize but only with a few; not willing to give himself up to it altogether. But if the studies of the Greeks delight you so much, there are others freer and more easily diffused, which we may bring to the use of life, or even to that of the republic. As for these arts, their value consists, if in any thing, in stimulating and sharpening the genius of young boys; enabling them in this manner the better to comprehend greater things.

XIX. "I do not dissent from you, Lælius," said Tubero, "but ask what you understand by greater things?"

Lælius. "I will tell you in good faith, although you may somewhat despise me for it; since it is you who are asking Scipio about these celestial matters. As for myself, I think those things most worthy of our attention, which lay immediately before our eyes. How can it interest me that the grandson of L. Paulus by the mother's side, born of such a noble and illustrious family in this republic, should seek for reasons why two suns have been seen, when he does not inquire the cause why two senates, and almost two people exist in one republic? For as you perceive the death of Tiberius Gracchus, and even before that event, the whole proceedings of his tribunate were dividing one people into two parties: those who are the detractors of Scipio also, and are envious of him, urged on at first by P. Crassus and Appius Claudius, keep up notwithstanding their death, an opposition to us in the senate, through the influence of Metellus and P. Mucius. Nor will they suffer him to come forward, who is alone equal to so dangerous a crisis, amidst the factious and dangerous associations made under the Roman name: amidst violated compacts, and the new matters daily stirring by the seditious triumvirs, to the consternation of good and respectable men. Wherefore young men, if you will listen to me, entertain no apprehensions about this double sun: for either it is nothing at all, or if it is a reality, as far as it has been observed, there is nothing injurious in it. Either we can know nothing about such matters, or even if we could know all about them, we should not be better or happier for that knowledge. But one senate and one people we may have; that is practicable. And if it is not done, we shall suffer for it. And we know it is otherwise, and that if it were effected, we should have more stability, and be happier and better."

XX. Then Mucius. "What is it we have to learn, in your opinion, Lælius, that we may be able to effect what you require of us?"

Lælius. "Those sciences whose tendency is to enable us to be useful to the state; for I deem that to be the most pre-eminent gift of wisdom, as well as the noblest fruit of virtue and duty. Wherefore that these holidays may be productive of conversations in an especial manner useful to the republic, let us entreat Scipio to impart to us, what he deems to be the happiest condition of a state. Afterwards we can consider other matters, the knowledge of which I hope will bring us to the subject before us, and will unfold the causes of the present condition of things.

[Two pages wanting.]

XXI. * * * * * not for that cause alone I wished it, but because I thought it proper that the first person in the republic should first speak on public affairs; and because I remembered that you were accustomed 62frequently to discuss with Panætius before Polybius, two Greeks extremely versed in civil affairs; and that you had proved by various reasonings the excellence of that form of government, which our ancestors had transmitted to us from so distant a period. In the which matter, you, being more competent to it, will do an agreeable thing to us all, (for I speak also for the rest,) if you will unfold to us your opinion of the commonwealth."

XXII. "I cannot," he began, "say that I have been in the habit of turning my mind more intensely and diligently to the consideration of any subject, than the very one which you now propose to me, Lælius. For when I perceive that every artificer who truly excels in his vocation, is filled with anxiety, care, and zeal, lest any one should surpass him in his art. I, whose chief duty, bequeathed to me by my parents and ancestors, is the conduct and administration of the republic, must confess myself more indolent than any artisan, if I bestowed less attention on the greatest of arts, than he does on the most insignificant. But neither am I satisfied with the writings on this subject which the first and wisest among the Greeks have left to us; while I hesitate to establish my own conclusions in preference to theirs. Wherefore I intreat you, not to listen to me as one entirely ignorant of the affairs of the Greeks, nor as one who gives them the preference to our own writers, particularly in matters of this kind; but as one liberally brought up by the diligence of distinguished parents, and ardent in the love of knowledge from his 63youth; yet nevertheless much more formed by domestic experience, than by literary studies."

XXIII. "I doubt," said Philus here, "whether any one has ever excelled you in genius. We know to what studies you have always been partial, and that in your acquaintance with the great affairs of the state, you have surpassed every one: wherefore if as you say, your mind has been particularly turned to matters which have now become almost a science: I feel very much indebted to Lælius, feeling a hope that what you will say will be more instructive, than all those things which the Greeks have written for us." "You are creating" replied he, "much expectation from my discourse, which is a very great weight upon one, who is about to speak of matters of importance." "However great it may be," said Philus, "you will throw it off as you are accustomed to do; nor is there any danger that a dissertation from you on government will be deficient in any requisite."

XXIV. "I will do what you desire, as well as I am able," rejoined Scipio, "and will begin the discussion in conformity with the rule which I think ought to be observed in the examination of all things, if you would avoid error. That the name of the subject in discussion being agreed upon, the meaning of the name shall be defined. If this be found to be appropriate, the matter can be entered upon at once; for unless this be perfectly understood at first, we never can understand what we are disputing about. Wherefore since it is of the republic we are inquiring, let us first examine what that is we are inquiring about." Lælius having shown 64his acquiescence. "I do not intend, however," said

Africanus, "in a matter so clear and familiar, to begin with the very origin of things; the first conjunction of the sexes; then their progeny and descendants, as some of our learned men are accustomed to do: nor shall I go into continual definitions of terms—what they are—and how many varieties of them. When I address wise men, who in war and in peace, have taken a glorious part in the affairs of a great republic, I shall not expose myself in such a manner, that the very thing under discussion shall be more intelligible, than my own explanation of it. Neither do I take upon me to pursue the subject in every direction, as a master would: nor can I promise to do it so effectually, that no omission whatever shall escape me." "It is exactly such a discourse as you promise, that I am in expectation of," said Lælius.

XXV. "A republic or commonwealth then," said Scipio, "is the wealth or common interest of the people. Every assemblage of men however, gathered together without an object, is not the people, but only an assemblage of the multitude associated by common consent, for reciprocal rights, and reciprocal usefulness. The leading cause of this congregating, is not to be ascribed so much to his weakness, as to the social principle innate with man. Our species is not a solitary and wandering one, but is so created that even when enjoying the greatest affluence * * * *

[Two pages wanting.]
65XXVI. * * * * rather intuitive; for no original institution of the social state has been found, nor of the other moral virtues. These congregations therefore made for the purposes I have explained, established their first seat in some particular place for a residence. Which after being fortified by their labours and by its position, and fitted with temples and public squares, the re-union of dwellings constructed after this manner, they called a town or city. Every people therefore, formed by the assemblage of such a multitude as I have described, every city which is the settlement of a people, every commonwealth which as I have said, is the wealth of the people, must in order to be permanent, be governed by some authority. That authority however must always have a strong relation to the causes from whence the commonwealth derived its origin. It may then be delegated to one, or to some selected persons; or it may be borne by the whole multitude of the people. When therefore authority over all things, is in the control of one man, we call him king; and a commonwealth so ordered, his kingdom. When the authority is exercised by selected persons, then such a state is said to be under the government of the better class. But there is also a popular form of government, for so it is called, where all things are ruled by the people. And of any of these three modes, if the chain is in any manner kept together, which at first united men into the social pact for the sake of the common interest, I would not indeed call the mode perfect, nor say that in my opinion it was the best, but that it was to be tolerated, and that one might 66be preferable to another. For whether under a just and wise king, or chosen eminent citizens, or the people themselves, although this last is least to be approved of, setting aside the irregularities occasioned by the bad passions of some men, any one may see that a steady government might be preserved.

XXVII. In kingdoms however, the governed are too much deprived of common rights, and of power. Under the better class, the multitude can scarcely be partakers of liberty, as they are not admitted either to the public councils or offices: and when the government is conducted by the people, although it be justly and moderately administered, yet equality itself becomes injustice, seeing that it admits of no degrees of rank. Therefore, although

Cyrus the Persian, was a most just and wise king, yet such a commonwealth, (for as I said before, it is the common property,) governed by the nod of one man, does not appear to me very desirable. And although the Massilians our clients are governed with great justice, by their chosen chief men, nevertheless in that condition of a people, there is something resembling slavery. And the Athenians at a certain period having abolished the Areopagus, conducted every thing by ordinances, and decrees of the people; yet as they had no distinctions in dignity, their state was without its ornament.

XXVIII. And this I say of these three kinds of government, not of the agitations and disturbances incidental to them, but of their tranquil and regular state. Those varieties are principally remarkable for the defects I have alluded to. Then they have other pernicious failings, for every one of these governments is travelling a dangerous road, bordering on a slippery and precipitous path. To a king so commendable, or if you choose, since I especially name him; to the amiable Cyrus; a parallel springs up in the cruel Phalaris, with all his capricious tyranny; into whose similitude the government of one man so easily slides with a downward course. To the administration of the city of the Massilians by their select chiefs, may be opposed the plot and faction of the Thirty, which took place at a certain period among the Athenians. Nor need we look farther; the very Athenian people having assumed the power over all things, and giving license to the fury of the multitude * * * * * *

[Two pages wanting.]
XXIX. * * * * * * and this great mischief arises whether under the rule of the better class, or under a tyrannical faction, or under the regal government; and even frequently under the popular form. At the same time from the various forms of government of which I have spoken, something excellent is wont to emanate. For the changes and vicissitudes in public affairs, appear to move in a circle of revolutions; which when recognized by a wise man, as soon as he beholds them impending, if he can moderate their course in the administration of affairs, and restrain them under his control; he acts truly the part of a great citizen, and almost of a divine man. Therefore I think a fourth kind of government, moderated and mixed from those three of which I first spoke, is most to be approved."

XXX. "I know" said Lælius, "that such is your opinion Africanus, for I have often heard you say so. Nevertheless, unless it is troublesome to you, I should be glad to learn which you judge best of these three kinds of government. For either it will throw some light upon * * * * * *

[Two pages wanting.]
XXXI. * * * * * * every government partakes of the nature and will of him who administers it. So that in no other state, save where the power of the people predominates, has liberty any home. Liberty the sweetest of all blessings, and which if it is not equal for all, is not liberty. For what equality can there be, I do not mean in kingdoms where slavery has no doubtful character: but in those states where all are nominally free: there indeed they give their votes, confer commands, magistracies and are solicited and intreated. But in truth they only part with that, however repugnant it may be to them, which must be conferred: things which they cannot retain, which is the reason why others seek to possess them. For they are invested with no command, have no public authority, nor are called to be judges in the tribunals: privileges which belong either to ancient

families, or are purchased by money. Among a free people however, as at Rhodes or Athens, there is no citizen who * * * * *

[Two pages wanting.]
69XXXII. Some assert, that when one or more in a state becomes conspicuous by his opulence or riches, disdain and pride soon break out: and the weak and indolent yield and bend under the arrogance of riches. But if the people are able to preserve their rights, they think no condition of things could be more excellent, more free, or more happy. For in their hands would be the laws, the tribunals, war, peace, treaties, and the properties and lives of all the citizens. This sort of government they think is properly called one republic, that is the common interest of the people. Wherefore it is, that the people are wont to restore commonwealths to liberty from the domination of kings, and patricians; not that kings are believed to be necessary to a free people, or that the better class are the source of power and wealth. And they deny that these advantages should not be conceded to a free people on account of the excesses of uncivilized nations: for where the people are unanimous, and every thing tends to the public safety and liberty, nothing can be more unchangeable, nothing more firm. Unanimity in such a commonwealth is very easy, where the common effort is for the public good. But from opposing interests, where one man clashes with another, discord arises. Wherefore when the senate had possession of the government, the condition of the state was never sound. In kingdoms the disadvantages are still greater; of them Ennius said

"No holy confidence or fellowship reigns there."
Wherefore as the law is the bond of civil society, and equal rights form that of the law, by what power can a 70community of citizens be maintained, where their condition is not an equal one? If therefore it is not expedient to equalize fortunes; if the powers of mind cannot be equalized in all, certainly then an equality of rights ought to exist, among those who are citizens of the same republic. For what is a state but a community of rights? * * * * *

[Two pages wanting.]
XXXIII. * * other governments however are deemed by them not to deserve those names, which they have chosen to arrogate to themselves. For why should I call a man who is greedy of rule, or of the sole command, and who is trampling upon an oppressed people, king, which is the title of the good Jupiter, rather than tyrant? A tyrant may be clement as well as a king may be oppressive; the matter really interesting to the people is, whether they are to serve under a gentle or a severe master: for as to being any thing but servants, that is not to be avoided. How could Lacedemon, when she was thought to excel in the science of government, possess only good and just kings, when she was obliged to take any king who was sprung from the royal blood? And the better class, who can endure them, who have arrogated to themselves in their own assemblies, a name not conceded to them by the people? For who is the man to be pronounced best, in learning, in the arts, in studies? * * * * *

[Four pages wanting.]
71XXXIV. * * * * If it was done by lot, the government would be overthrown; like a ship, at whose helm, some passenger taken at hazard was placed. A nation can entrust its affairs to whom it may choose; and if it wishes to remain free, it will choose from among the best. For certainly the security of states is found in the counsels of the best citizens;

especially as nature has not only ordained that they should preserve an influence over the weak by their conspicuous virtue and courage, but also that the weak should resign themselves to the government of great minds. This most desirable state of things, they say, is prevented by the erroneous opinions of men who, through ignorance of that virtue, which belongs to but few, and is seen and appreciated only by few, deem those who are sprung from a noble race, or who are opulent and wealthy, to be the best men. Under this vulgar error, when the power, not the virtues of a few, have got possession of the government; those chiefs tenaciously preserve the title of better class; a name however to which the substance is wanting. For riches, titles, and power, devoid of wisdom, of the knowledge of self-government, and that of the government of others, exhibit nothing but insolent and disgraceful pride. Nor can the condition of any city be more deplorable, than where the richest men pass for the best. But what can be more delightful than a state virtuously governed? What more illustrious than the man, who while he governs others, is himself the slave of no bad passions? Who, while he calls upon the citizens to observe the regulations he has formed, lives up to them all himself? Nor imposes any laws 72upon the people, which he himself obeys not, but who presents his whole life to his fellow citizens as one unbroken law. If one man could suffice to all things, there would be no need of many; and if all men could perceive what is best, and consent to it, no one would require any chiefs to be elected. The difficulty of coming to wise determinations, has transferred the rule from one king to many persons; and the error and rashness of the people, from the multitude to a few. Thus between the obstinacy of one, and the temerity of many, the better class have possessed themselves of the middle and least turbulent of all the situations: by whom if the commonwealth is well administered, the people relieved from all care and thought, must necessarily be happy: enjoying their independence through the labours of those, whose duty it is to preserve it to them; and who ought never to permit the people to think that their interests are neglected by their rulers. As to that exact equality of rights, which is held so dear by a free people; it cannot be preserved: for the people themselves, however free and unrestrained they may be, are remarkable for their deference to many persons; and exercise a great preference as it respects men and dignities. That which is called equality also, is a most unjust thing in itself: for when the same honour is enjoyed by the high and by the low, through a whole people, that very equality must be unjust; and in those states which are governed by the better class, it can never happen. These, Lælius, and some other reasons resembling them, are wont to be urged by those who chiefly praise that form of government.

73XXXV. "But which, Scipio, among those three, do you chiefly approve of?" said Lælius.

Scipio. "You do well to ask, which chiefly of the three, since separately I do not approve of any of them; but should prefer to every one of them, a government constituted out of all three. But if one of them for its simplicity may be admired, I should approve of the kingly form, and give it the highest praise. For the name of king calls up at once the idea of a father, consulting with his citizens as if they were his own children; and more anxious to preserve them, than to reduce them to slavery: it being a great advantage to the weak to be sustained by the exertions and by the foresight of one pre-eminent and good man. Here however the better class profess to do the same thing to more advantage, and say there is more wisdom with numbers than with one, and at the same time equal justice and faith. But the people call out with a loud voice, that they choose neither to obey one nor many; that nothing is sweeter to the beasts of the field than liberty, which is wanting to all who serve either under the better class or under a king. Thus on the score of personal attachment, kings attract us. The better class by their wisdom; and liberty on the side of the people. So that in making the comparison, it is difficult to say which is preferable."

L. "I believe it," said he, "but if you leave this point unfinished, the other parts of the subject can scarcely be cleared up."

XXXVI. S. "Let us imitate therefore Aratus, who in his introduction to a discourse upon high matters, thought it best to begin with Jupiter."

74L. "Why with Jupiter? and what has this discussion to do with the verses of Aratus?"

S. "Insomuch, that the opening of our debate may be honoured with the name of him, whom all, learned and unlearned, consent with one voice, to be the one king of all the gods and men." "What then!" said Lælius. "What do you believe in but the things which are before your eyes?" replied he. "This opinion has been established for the conduct of life, by those who have had the direction of public affairs; that the belief might prevail, that one king ruled in heaven, who with his nod, as Homer says, could tumble down Olympus; and that he should be considered as the King and Father of all. Great is the authority for it, and many the witnesses, inasmuch as all have concurred in it. Nations too have agreed, as we find in the decrees of princes, that the regal form of government was most excellent, since they imagine the gods themselves to be under the government of one king. And if we have been told that this and similar opinions have sprung from fables and the errors of the ignorant, let us listen to those who may be considered almost the common teachers of erudite men; who as it were, saw these very things with their eyes, which we scarcely are acquainted with, when we hear of them." "And who are they?" said Lælius. "They," replied he, who in their investigations of the nature of all things, have perceived a design in the universal structure of this world * * * * * *

[Four pages wanting.]
75XXXVII. * * * * * * "But if you desire it Lælius, I can give you authorities in no wise barbarous, nor of too remote an antiquity."

L. I should be glad to have them.

S. You are aware that it is now somewhat less than four hundred years since this city has been governed without kings.

L. That is true; rather less.

S. What then are four hundred years, for the age of a city or state; is it such a long period?

L. It can hardly be called an adult age.

S. Then there was a king in Rome four hundred years ago?

L. And a very superb one.

S. Who before him?

L. A most just one; and from that period up to Romulus, who reigned six hundred years from the present time.

S. Then he is not so very remote.

L. Not at all. The institutions of Greece were already on the wane.

S. I submit to you now, whether Romulus was the king of a barbarous people?

L. If as the Greeks say, all men were either Greeks or Barbarians; then I am afraid he must be esteemed a king of a barbarous people. But if that epithet is appropriate to a difference of manners, rather than to languages, I think the Greeks not less barbarians than the Romans." "In relation to the matter of which we speak," said Scipio, "it is intelligence we are looking for, rather than men. If a discreet people therefore, not of 76a very ancient period, have preferred the government of kings, I am availing myself of testimony which cannot be deemed savage, uncivilized, or of a barbarous antiquity."

XXXVIII. "I perceive Scipio," said Lælius, "that you are sufficiently provided with testimony. But with me, as with good judges, sound argument prevails more than witnesses." "Make use of an argument then," replied Scipio, "which your knowledge of yourself can suggest to you." "What knowledge," said he.

S. Why as when by chance it happens to you to be angry with some one.

L. That occurs oftener than I could wish.

S. What! when you are in anger, do you suffer your mind to fall under the domination of that passion?

L. No, so help me Hercules. I rather imitate Archytas, the Tarentine; who on arriving at his country house, and being greatly offended at perceiving his orders had been disobeyed, "You are a miserable wretch," said he to his farmer, "and I would have you flogged to death if I were not angry." "Excellent," said Scipio. "Archytas wished to calm his anger by reflection, considering that degree of it which was not under the control of reason, to be leading on to a sort of sedition of the mind. To it add avarice, ambition, the passion for glory, and for sensual pleasures; and it will appear that there exists in the minds of men, a sort of regal controlling power, to wit, reflection. For that is the best part of the mind, and where its authority 77prevails, there is no room for sensuality, for anger, or for rashness.

L. So it is.

S. Do you approve therefore of a mind so disposed?

L. There is nothing I admire more.

S. Then you really do not think, reflection being driven away; that voluptuousness or the angry passions, which are without end, should have the mastery in all things.

L. Indeed I can conceive of nothing more wretched, than such a state of mind; nor of a man more debased than when under such government.

S. You prefer then all parts of the mind, to be under some government, the government of reflection?

L. I certainly prefer it.

S. Why therefore do you hesitate in your opinion about public affairs; where if the administration is transferred to many, there will be no one, as I now understand it, to take the command. And it seems that if authority is not one thing, it is nothing at all.

XXXIX. "I would ask," said Lælius, "of what consequence it is to us, whether one or many, if justice is dispensed by the latter." "Since I find Lælius," said Scipio, "that my witnesses have made no great impression on you, I shall not desist from making use of yourself as a witness to prove what I say." "Me," said he, "in what way?"

S. Why adverting to the directions you so earnestly gave to your family, when we were lately at Formianum; to obey only the orders of one person.

78L. Oh! my farmer!

S. Well, at home, I suppose, several are entrusted with the management of your affairs?

L. No, only one.

S. What, your whole establishment! does no one but yourself manage it?

L. Just so.

S. Do not you therefore accede to the same conclusion in public affairs: that the government of a single person, if it is a just one, is the best?

L. I am brought to the conclusion, and must almost assent to it.

XL. You will be more inclined to that opinion, said Scipio, when omitting the analogies of one pilot, one physician, who if they are any way skilled in their arts, ought one to have the control of the ship; the other of the patient, in preference to many; I come to the consideration of greater matters.

L. What are they?

S. Are you not aware that the name of king became odious to this people, on account of the oppression and pride of one man, Tarquin?

L. Yes, I am aware.

S. Then you are aware of what haply in the course of this discussion, I may find occasion to speak. Tarquin being driven out, the people exulted with a marvellous sort of insolence of freedom. At one time driving innocent people into exile; at another, confiscating the property of many. Next came annual consuls. Then the fasces prostrated before the people—appeals in all cases. Then the mutiny of the plebeians—then 79a complete revolution in every thing, placing all things in the power of the people.

L. It is as you say. "It is true," said Scipio—"in peace and tranquillity, some license may be permitted when there is nothing to fear, as at sea sometimes, or in a slight fever: but like him who is at sea, when suddenly the ocean puts on its terrors, or the sick man, when his complaint oppresses him, and the assistance of one is implored: so our people in time of peace, interfere in internal affairs, threaten the magistrates, refuse submission to them, denounce them and provoke them; yet in war obey them as they would a king, preferring their safety to the indulgence of their passions. Also in our more important wars, our countrymen have constantly preferred the command to be in the hands of one, without any colleague; the extent of whose power is indicated by his name. For a dictator is so called on account of every thing being dictated by him. But in our books, Lælius, you see also that he is called master of the people."

L. It is so. "Wisely therefore did those ancients," said Scipio * * * *

[Two pages wanting.]
XLI. * * * When a people is deprived of a just king, as Ennius says, after the death of one of the best of kings,

"Long were their bosoms moved with deep regret;
Oft they together call upon his manes.
Oh, godlike Romulus! the bounteous gods
80What a protector did they give in thee?
Oh father, parent, blood derived from heaven!"
Those whom the laws enjoined them to obey, they did not call lords or masters; finally, not even kings, but guardians of the country, fathers and gods. Nor without cause, for what is added,

"Thou broughtest us into the realms of light!"
They thought that life, honour, and every comfort was given to them by the justice of a king. And the same inclinations would have remained with their posterity, if the character of their kings had not changed. But you perceive that kind of government was ruined by the injustice of one man.

L. I do perceive it, and I am desirous of knowing the course of these changes, not only in our own country, but in all governments.

XLII. "It will be for you," said Scipio, "when I shall have given my opinion of that kind of government which I prefer, to give a more accurate account of the mutations in governments; although I do not think them much to be apprehended in the form I am inclined to. But a regal form of government is particularly and most certainly exposed to change. When a king begins to be unjust, that form of government perishes at once. The tyrant is, at the same time, the worst of all conditions of government, and the nearest to the best. Whom, if the better class have overturned, which for the most part happens, the commonwealth possesses 81that second class of the three. And this is a sort of royalty; a paternal government of the principal people, for the benefit of the rest. But if the people cast out or slay the tyrant; rejoicing in their own deed, they are more moderate, as long as they know and feel the value of being so, in their endeavour to protect the commonwealth constituted by themselves. But when the populace have bent their force against a just king, and have stripped him of his kingdom; or even, as it happens very often, have tasted the blood of the better class, and have prostrated the whole republic in their madness; think not that the vexed ocean or the wildest conflagration, can be more easily kept down, than the unbridled insolence of the multitude.

XLIII. Then is produced what in Plato is so clearly described, if I can in any manner express it in Latin, a thing difficult to be done, but I will endeavour. "It is then," he says, "when the insatiable throats of the people, parched with the thirst of liberty, and led on by rash demagogues, have greedily drank, not temperate but too unalloyed draughts of freedom. Then the magistrates and chiefs, unless they are too lenient and indulgent, permitting them every excess of liberty; are pursued, impeached, insulted, and called oppressors, kings, and tyrants." I think this part of his works is known to you.

L. I am well acquainted with it.

S. Then follows, "Those who pay obedience to the magistrates, are tormented by the people, are called voluntary slaves. But those magistrates who affect to be on an equality with the lowest; and other individuals 82who strive to abolish all distinction between citizens and magistrates, are exalted with praises, and overwhelmed with honours. And in this condition of things, it follows, of course, that there is an unrestrained license in a government of this kind; so that every private family is without any government: and this evil extends even to the beasts. At length the father fears the son—the son disregards the father: every sort of decency is extinguished, that an open license may prevail. Nothing distinguishes the citizen from the stranger. The master pays court to his scholars, that he may be flattered by them. Teachers are despised by their disciples. Young persons take upon themselves the authority of aged ones, who abase themselves to mingle in their games, lest they become odious and burdensome to them. At last slaves give themselves all sorts of liberties. Wives assume the privileges of their husbands. Nay the dogs, the horses, the asses at length are so infected with liberty, and run kicking about so, that it is absolutely necessary to get out of their way. Wherefore from this infinite license these things result, that the minds of the citizens become so scornful and impatient, that if the least power of government is exercised, they become exasperated and will not endure it; whence they come to despise every kind of law, that they may be without the least restraint whatever."

XLIV. "You have," said Lælius, "precisely expressed Plato's sentiments."

S. Returning therefore to the subject of my discourse. "It is from this very license," he says, "which they deem to be liberty itself, that a tyrant 83springs up as a sapling from a root. For as the destruction of the better class arises from their overweening power, so this excess of liberty, effects the slavery of this free people. Thus all extremes of an agreeable nature, whether in the seasons, or in the fertility of the fields, or in our natural feelings, are often converted into their opposites. Especially it occurs in public affairs, where excess of liberty degenerates into public and individual slavery. Out of such licentious freedom a tyrant arises, and the most unjust and severe bondage. For by a people so untameable, or rather so outrageous, some leader is chosen out of the multitude, in opposition to the better class, now persecuted and driven from their offices: bold and dishonest, perversely persecuting those who have frequently deserved well of their country, and gratifying the people from his own means and from those of others. To whom, that he may be freed from all apprehensions on account of his private condition, authority is given and continued to him. Surrounded too by guards, as was the case with Pisistratus at Athens, at length he becomes the tyrant of the very citizens who brought him forward. Who, if he is subdued by the good, as often happens, the state is regenerated. If by the bad, then a faction is established, another kind of tyranny. The same state of things too frequently occurs in that goodly form of government of the better class, when the vices of the chiefs have caused them to deviate from their integrity. Thus do they snatch the government of the commonwealth from each other like a ball—tyrants from kings—chiefs or the people from 84tyrants; and factions or tyrants from them, nor does the same mode of government ever last a long time.

XLV. These things being so, the regal form of government is in my opinion much to be preferred of those three kinds. Nevertheless one which shall be well tempered and balanced out of all those three kinds of government, is better than that; yet there should be always something royal and pre-eminent in a government, at the same time that some power should be placed in the hands of the better class, and other things reserved for the judgment and will of the multitude. Now we are struck first with the great equability of such a constitution, without which a people cannot be free long; next with its stability. The three other kinds of government easily fall into the contrary extremes: as a master grows out of a king; factions from the better class; and mobs and confusion from the people. The changes too are perpetual which are taking place. This cannot well happen in such a combined and moderately balanced government, unless by the great vices of the chief persons. For there is no cause for change, where every one is firmly placed in his proper station, and never gives way, whatever may fall down or be displaced.

XLVI. But I am afraid, Lælius, and you too my very discreet and respected friends, if I continue long in this strain, my discourse will appear more like that of a master or teacher to you, than as a conversation with you. Wherefore I will speak of matters known to us all, and which we have all inquired into long ago. For I am convinced, and believe, and declare, that no kind 85of government, either in the constitution, the planning, or the practice, is to be compared with that which our fathers have left to us, and which was adopted by our ancestors. Which if you please, since you have been desirous that I should repeat things known to yourselves, I will shew not only what it is, but that it is the best. And with our own government in view, I will if I can, have a reference to it, in whatever I may say respecting the best form of government. The which if I can follow up and effect, I shall, as I think, amply fulfil the task which Lælius has imposed on me.

XLVII. "It is your task indeed, Scipio," said Lælius, "most truly yours. For who in preference to yourself may speak of the institutions of our forefathers; you being sprung from such illustrious ancestors; or of the best form of government. The which if we now possess it, would hardly be so, if any one stood in a more conspicuous situation than yourself. Or who may venture to advise measures for posterity, when thou, having delivered the city from its greatest terrors, hast foreseen for the latest times?"

CICERO'S REPUBLIC.

BOOK II.

I. Perceiving them all now eager to listen to him, Scipio thus began to speak. "It was old Cato, to whom as you know I was singularly attached, and whom I admired in the highest degree: to whom, either through the advice of both my parents, or from my own prepossession, I devoted myself entirely from my youth; whose conversation never could satiate me. Such was the experience of the man in public affairs, which he had for a long time successfully conducted in peace and war. His manner of speaking too, a facetiousness mixed with gravity: his constant desire also to improve himself and others; indeed his whole life in harmony with his maxims. He was wont to say, that the condition of our country was pre-eminent above all others for this cause. That among other people, individuals generally had respectively constituted the government by their laws and by their institutes, as Minos in Crete, Lycurgus in Lacedemon. At Athens, where the changes were frequent, at first Theseus, then Draco, then Solon, then Clisthenes; afterwards many others. Finally exhausted and prostrated, it had been upheld by 88that learned man Demetrius, of Phalera. But that the constitution of our republic was not the work of one, but of many; and had not been established in the life of one man, but during several generations and ages. For he said so powerful a mind had never existed; from which nothing had escaped; nor that all minds collected into one, could foresee so much at one time, as to comprehend all things without the aid of practice and time. For which reason, as he was wont, so shall my discourse now repeat the origin of the people; for I have a pleasure in using the very words of Cato. But I shall more easily follow up my proposition in describing our own republic to you, in its infancy, its growth, in its adult, and its present firm and robust state; than if I were to create an imaginary one, as Socrates is made to do in Plato.

II. When all had approved of this, he proceeded. "What beginning, therefore, have we of the establishment of a republic so illustrious and so known to you all, as the origin of the building of this city by Romulus, born of his father Mars? For let us concede to the common opinion of men, especially as it is not only well established, but also wisely recorded by our ancestors, that those who have deserved well of us on account of our common interest, be deemed not only to have possessed a divine genius, but also a divine origin. He therefore after his birth, with Remus his brother, is said to have been ordered to be exposed on the Tiber, by the Alban king, Amulius, apprehensive lest his kingdom should be shaken. In which place, having been sustained by the teats of a wild beast, the shepherds 89took him, and brought him up in the labour and cultivation of the fields. It is said, that when he had grown up, he was distinguished above the rest by his corporeal strength, and the daringness of his mind. So that all who then inhabited the fields, where at this day stands the city, obeyed him willingly and without dissent. And being constituted their leader, that we may now come from fables to facts, with a strong force he took Alba-longa, a powerful and well constructed city in those times, and put the king Amulius to death.

III. Having acquired which glory, he is said first to have auspiciously thought of building a city, and of establishing a government. In regard to the situation of the city, a circumstance which is most carefully to be considered by him, who endeavours to establish a permanent government; he chose it with incredible skill. For neither did he remove to the sea, although it was a very easy thing for him with his forces, to march through the territory of the Rutulians and Aborigines; neither would he build a city at the mouth of the Tiber, to which place the king Ancus led a colony many years after. For he perceived, with an admirable foresight, that maritime situations were not proper for those cities which were founded in the hope of continuance, or with a view to empire. First, because maritime towns were not only exposed to many dangers, but to unseen ones. For the ground over which an expected enemy moves, as well as an unexpected one, announces his approach beforehand by many indications: by sound itself of a peculiarly tumultuous kind. No enemy can make a march, however forced, without our not only knowing 90him to be there, but even who he is, and whence he comes. But a maritime enemy and a naval force may be before you, ere any one can suspect him to be come. Nor even when he does come, does he carry before him any indication of who he is, or from whence he comes, or even what he wants. Finally by no kind of sign can it be discerned or determined whether he is a friend or an enemy.

IV. In maritime cities, too, a sort of debasing and changeable manners prevail. New languages and new customs are mingled together, and not only productions but manners are imported from abroad; so that nothing remains entire of the pristine institutions. Even they who inhabit those cities are not faithful to their homes, but with capricious inclinations and longings are carried far from them; and although their persons remain, their minds are rambling and wandering abroad. Nor did Carthage or Corinth, long before shaken, owe their ruin to any thing more than to the unsettled scattering of the citizens, who abandoned the study of agriculture and arms through their cupidity of gain and love of roaming. Many pernicious excitements too to luxury, are brought over the sea to cities by commercial importation or by conquest. Even the very amenity of the situation suggests many costly and enervating allurements. What I have said of Corinth, I know not if I may as truly say of all Greece; for almost all Peloponnesus lies on the sea, and except the Phliuntians, there are none whose lands do not extend to the coast. Beyond Peloponnesus, the Enianes, the Dorians, and the Dolopians are the only people in the interior. 91What shall I say of the islands of Greece? which surrounded with billows, float about as it were with the institutions and manners of their cities. These things as I said before, relate to ancient Greece; but of the colonies brought by the Greeks into Asia, Thrace, Italy, Sicily, and Africa, except Magnesia alone, which of them is not washed by the ocean? Thus a part of the Grecian shores seemed to be joined to the lands of the barbarians. For among the barbarians themselves, none were a maritime people, except the Etruscans and the Carthagenians; the one for the sake of commerce, the other for the sake of piracy. A most obvious cause of the evils and revolutions of Greece, arising from the vices of these maritime cities, which awhile ago I slightly touched upon. Nevertheless among these evils there is a great convenience. The products of every distant nation can be wafted to the city you inhabit; and in return the productions of your own lands can be sent or carried into whatever countries you choose.

V. Who then more inspiredly than Romulus could secure all the maritime conveniences, and avoid all the defects? placing the city on the banks of a perennial river, broadly flowing with an equal course to the sea. By which the city might receive what it wanted from the ocean, and return whatever was superfluous. Receiving by the same channel all things essential to the wants and the refinements of life, not only from the sea, but likewise from the interior. So that it appears to me, he had foreseen this city, at some period, would be the seat and capital of a mighty empire: for a city placed in any other part of Italy would not easily have been able to acquire such a powerful influence.

VI. As to the native defences of the city, who is so unobservant as not to have them marked and fixed in his mind? Such is the alignment and direction of the wall, which by the wisdom of Romulus, as well of succeeding kings, was bounded on every part by lofty and craggy hills: so that the only entrance, which was between the Esquiline and the Quirinal hills, was defended by a huge mound, and a very wide ditch. The citadel, surrounded by this craggy and seemingly hewn rock, had such a gallant position, that in that furious invasion of the terrible Gauls, it remained safe and intact. He choose also a place abounding in springs, and salubrious even in a pestilent region. For there are hills which while they enjoy the breezes, at the same time throw a cool shade upon the vallies.

VII. These things were done too with great celerity. For he not only founded a city, which he ordered to be called Rome, from his own name; but to establish it, and strengthen the power of the people and his kingdom, he adopted a strange and somewhat clownish plan, but worthy of a great man, whose providence extended far into futurity. When the Sabine virgins, descended from respectable families, were come to Rome to see the games, whose first anniversary he had then ordered to be celebrated in the circus, he ordered them to be seized during the sports, and gave them in marriage to the most honourable families. For which cause, when the Sabines had made war upon the Romans, and when the success of the battle was various and doubtful, he struck a league with Tatius, king of the Sabines, at the entreaty of the very matrons who had been seized: in consequence of which he admitted the Sabines into the city: and mutually having embraced each others sacred rites, he associated their king with him in the government.

VIII. After the death however of Tatius, all the power came back into his hands: although he had admitted some chiefs into the royal council with Tatius, who were called fathers, on account of the affection borne to them. He also divided the people into three tribes, named after himself, after Tatius, and after Lucumon, a companion of Romulus, who had been slain in the Sabine war: and into thirty curia, which curia he called by the names of those from among the Sabine virgins seized, at whose entreaties the peace and league had been formed. But although these things were done before the death of Tatius, yet after that event, his government became much better established, aided by the authority and counsel of the fathers.

IX. In the which he saw and judged as Lycurgus at Sparta had done, a little while before him: that states were better governed by individual command and royal power, if the authority of some of the better class were added to the energy of that kind of government. Thus sustained, and as it were propped up by the senatorial authority, he carried on many wars very successfully with his neighbours; and appropriating to himself no part of the spoil, he never ceased to enrich the citizens. At that time Romulus paid in most things attention to auspices, a custom we still retain, and greatly advantageous to the republic. For he built the city under the observance of auspices at the very beginning of the republic; and in the establishment of all public affairs, he chose an augur from each of the tribes to assist him in the auspices. He also had the common people assigned as clients to the principal men, the utility of which measure I will afterwards consider. Fines were paid in sheep and cattle: for then all property consisted in flocks, and in possessions of lands, whence the terms pecuniary[12] and landholders[13] were derived. He did not attempt to govern by severity or the infliction of punishments.

X. When Romulus had reigned thirty-seven years, and had established those two excellent foundations of the state, the auspices and the senate, he obtained this great meed: for when he had disappeared upon a sudden obscuration of the sun, he was deemed to have been placed among the number of the gods. A belief which no mortal had ever inspired without the greatest pre-eminence in virtue. And this is most to be admired in Romulus, that others who are said to have been deified out of the mortal state, lived in the less civilized ages of man, when the proneness to fiction was great, and the unenlightened were easily led to believe in it. But during the period of Romulus, not quite six hundred years ago, we know that learning and literature existed, and that the ancient errors peculiar to the uncultivated ages of mankind were removed. For if Rome, according to an investigation of the annals of the Greeks, was built in the second year of the seventh olympiad; the reign of Romulus occurred at that period when Greece 95was full of poets and musicians; and when but little faith would be given to fabulous stories, unless they were concerning very ancient things. For one hundred and eight years after Lycurgus ordained laws to be written, the first olympiad was established: which through a mistake in the name, some have thought to be founded by Lycurgus. Homer, however, by those who take the lowest period, is made to precede Lycurgus about thirty years. From which it may be gathered that Homer flourished many years before Romulus. So that there was scarce room in so intelligent an age, and amid so many learned men, for any one to establish fictions. Antiquity sometimes has received fables crudely devised, but that age already refined, and especially deriding improbable events, has rejected * * *

[About 230 letters wanting.]
* * * * Simonides was born in the fifty-sixth olympiad, by which the credit given to the immortality of Romulus may be more easily understood, seeing that the institutions of society were then so well established, organized, and known. But really so great was the force of his genius and virtue, that what men would have given no credit to for many ages in favour of any other man, was believed of Romulus upon the evidence of Proculus Julius, a countryman, who at the instigation of the fathers, in order to repel from themselves every suspicion of the death of Romulus, is said to have declared in the assembly, that he had seen Romulus on that mount which is now called 96Quirinal; and that he had commanded him to request the people to erect a temple for him upon that hill; that he was a god, and was called Quirinus.

XI. "Do not you perceive therefore a new people not only sprung from the wisdom of one man, and not left crying in leading strings, but already grown up, and almost an adult?" "Indeed we perceive it," said Lælius, "and that you have entered upon a new method of discussion, which is no where to be found in the writings of the Greeks. For that pre-eminent person,[14] whom no one has excelled in writing, has imagined to himself a situation, in which he might construct his city after his own pleasure: admirable enough perhaps, but foreign to the conduct and the manners of men. Others have discussed the subject in relation to the kinds and causes of governments, but not under any particular example of a form of government. You seem to me to be about to do both, for according to your method, you appear to prefer to attribute to others what you yourself have observed, than to imagine a state of things, as Socrates is made to do in Plato. And these matters respecting the foundation of the city, you suppose to be part of a system, which were only adopted by Romulus through necessity or chance. And your discourse is not of a desultory kind, but concerning a particular commonwealth. Wherefore proceed as you have begun, for already I perceive you are about to follow on with the other kings, as perfecting the government."

XII. "Wherefore," said Scipio, "when the senate, 97which Romulus had instituted out of the better class, and which had been so much favoured by the king, as to cause them to be called fathers, and their children patricians; endeavoured after the death of Romulus, to carry on the government itself without any king; the people would not endure it, and in their regret for Romulus did not cease to demand a king. Upon which the leading men prudently imagined a mode of interregnum, new and unknown to other nations. So that until a regular king was proclaimed, neither the city should be without a king, nor with one too long a period. Fearing lest from too long an enjoyment of the government, the interrex should be reluctant to lay it down, or strong enough to maintain himself in it. Even in these times, this new people perceived what had escaped the Lacedemonian Lycurgus; who esteemed it best not to choose a king, if this were indeed in the power of Lycurgus to do, but rather to be governed by any one whatever descended from the race of Hercules. But our ancestors, rude as they appear to have been, thought it behoved them rather to look to royal wisdom and virtue, than to descent.

XIII. When the great fame of Numa Pompilius had reached them, the people, leaving aside their own citizens, called in by the authority of the fathers, a king not born among them, and sent to the Curians for a Sabine to reign over Rome. When he arrived, although the people had decided that he should be king in the conventions of the curia, nevertheless he himself had a law passed in the curia concerning his own power; and as he saw the Romans through the institutions of Romulus 98were eager after warlike pursuits, he deemed it proper to wean them somewhat from that propensity.

XIV. And first, the lands which Romulus had acquired in war, he divided equally among the citizens; and pointed out to them, that without depopulating and pillaging, they might possess all the necessaries of life, by the cultivation of their lands. He inspired them also with the love of peace and repose, under which justice and good faith most kindly flourish; and under the protection of which, the cultivation of the fields, and the gathering of the harvest are most secure. The same Pompilius having established auspices of a superior kind, added two augurs to the ancient number, and placed five priests over sacred things from the class of the chief men. And having established those laws which we possess in our monuments, he softened, by the ceremonies of religion, minds which were inflamed by the habit and inclination of making war. He added also Flamens, Salii, and Vestal Virgins; and established with great solemnity all the branches of religion: ordaining many ceremonies to be learnt and observed, but without any expense. Thus he increased the duty of religious observances and diminished the cost of them. In like manner he established markets, games, and all the stated occasions of assembling the people together. Under which institutions, he recalled the minds of men become fierce and wild in warlike pursuits, to humanity and gentleness. When he had reigned thirty-nine years in the most perfect peace and concord, (in this we follow principally our friend Polybius, than whom no one was more accurate in ascertaining 99periods,) he departed from life; having strengthened every thing for the endurance of the government, by those two conspicuous virtues, religion and clemency.

XV. When Scipio had spoken these words. "Is it true, Africanus," said Manilius, "what tradition has brought down to us, that this king Numa was a disciple of Pythagoras, or is it certain he was a Pythagorean? For often we have heard this, as having been declared by old people, and understand it also to be the common opinion; yet we do not see it sufficiently proved by the authority of the public annals." "It is false," replied Scipio, "entirely so Manilius! Not false alone, but ignorantly and absurdly false; for the mendacity of those assertions is not to be endured, which we not only see are not true, but which could never have been so. It was in the fourth year of the reign of Lucius Tarquinius Superbus, that Pythagoras is ascertained to have come to Sybaris and Crotona, and those parts of Italy. For the sixty-second Olympiad announces that very arrival of Pythagoras, and the beginning of the reign of Superbus. From which it may be understood by a calculation of the reigns, that Pythagoras touched first at Italy about a hundred and forty years after the death of Numa. Nor has this fact, by those who have very diligently investigated the annals of the times, ever been thrown into any doubt." "Immortal gods," said Manilius, "how inveterate and great is the error of men! Nevertheless, I can be very well pleased in the belief, that our intelligence has not been derived from abroad, and through foreign arts, but from natural and domestic virtues."

100 XVI. "You will distinguish that more clearly," said Africanus, "when you perceive how the commonwealth advances and comes to the greatest perfection by a straight forward and natural course. For in this also the wisdom of our ancestors is to be praised; that many things derived from abroad, have been rendered much more perfect by us, than they were from whence they were brought, and where they first had existence. You will see also that the greatness of the Roman people has not been confirmed by chance, but by wisdom and discipline. Fortune indeed being propitious to us.

XVII. King Pompilius being dead, the people upon the proposition of an interrex, created Tullus Hostilius king, in the conventions of the curia; and he, after the example of Pompilius, consulted the people in the curia, concerning his power. His military glory was great, and important warlike affairs took place. He constructed edifices for the senate and the curia, and surrounded them with military trophies. He established a law also for the declaration of war, which most justly decreed by him, he made more sacred by the solemnity of Heralds: so that every war which was not proclaimed and declared, was deemed to be impious and unjust. And observe how wisely our kings saw that some sort of deference must be paid to the people. I might say many things on that head. Tullus indeed did not venture to appear with royal insignia unless at the command of the people. For in order that it might be lawful for him to be preceded by twelve lictors with their fasces * *

[Two pages wanting.]

101 XVIII. * * * * * "The government which your discourse is establishing, does not creep, but rather flies towards perfection." S. "After him, Ancus Martius, grandson to Numa Pompilius by his daughter, was made king by the people, who had his elevation sanctioned by a law of the curia. Who having conquered the Latins in a war, incorporated them into the state. He also added the Aventine and Cælian Mounts to the city. The lands too which he had conquered he distributed, and made a public domain of all the forests he had taken on the sea coast. He built a city at the mouth of the Tiber, and planted a colony there. When he had thus reigned twenty-three years, he died. "This king also is to be praised," said Lælius, "but the Roman history is obscure: for although we know who

was the mother of this king, we do not know who was his father." S. "So it is" said he, "but generally the names of the kings only of those times are conspicuous."

XIX. "But it is here that we first perceive the city to have become more intelligent by extrinsic information. For not a gentle stream flowed from Greece into this city, but an abundant flood of arts and knowledge. It is stated that one Demaratus, a Corinthian, a principal man, and of much honour and authority in his own city, and of an easy fortune, not being able to endure Cypselus, the tyrant of the Corinthians, fled with a great deal of money, and betook himself to a flourishing city of Etruria, among the Tarquinians. When he had heard that the domination of Cypselus was confirmed, being an independent and powerful man, he renounced his country, and was received a citizen by the Tarquinians: and in that city he fixed his home and establishment. Where when he had begotten two sons from one of the Tarquinian matrons, he instructed them in all the arts after the manner of the Greeks * * * *

[Two pages wanting.]
XX. * * * * * He was well received in the city, and became intimate with king Ancus on account of his learning and liberal knowledge. So much so that he shared all his counsels, and might be deemed even a partner in his kingdom. For there was a great affability in him, and an extreme readiness in aiding, protecting, and doing liberal acts to every citizen. Martius therefore being dead, L. Tarquinius was created king by the united suffrages of the people; for thus he had changed his name from his Grecian one, that in every thing he might be seen to imitate the manners of the people. Having caused his accession to be confirmed by a law, he doubled the pristine number of the fathers; calling those whose opinions he first asked, ancient fathers of the greater families; and those whom he had admitted, he called the lesser families. Then he established the knights; after the manner that has obtained unto our day. He could not change the names of the Titienses, of the Rhamnensians, or the Luceres, when he wished to do so; because Attus Nævius being then Augur in great reputation, would not consent to it. We see the Corinthians chose formerly to assign cavalry for the public service, and to have their expenses defrayed by taxes on orphans and widows. But to the old troops of horse he added others, and made twelve hundred knights. He doubled this number after he had subdued the Equi in war, a powerful and ferocious race, which threatened the affairs of the Roman people. And when he had driven the Sabines from the walls of the city, he scattered them with his horse and conquered them. It is he whom we understand to have instituted the great games, which we call Roman, and to have made a vow during the Sabine war, while in battle, that he would raise a temple on the capitol to the great and good Jupiter. He died when he had reigned thirty-eight years.

XXI. "Now," said Lælius, "is that saying of Cato very certain, that the constitution of the state is not the work of one moment or one man: for it is evident how great an accession of good and useful institutions occurred under each reign. But he comes next, who appears to me to have looked farther than them all into the nature of government." "So it is," said Scipio, "for after him Servius Sulpicius is stated first to have reigned without the command of the people. He is said to have been born of a Tarquinian slave: she having conceived him by some client of the king. Brought up among the number of the servants, when he attended at the royal table, he did not suppress those sparks of genius, which even then shone forth in the boy: so shrewd was he in every thing, whether in business or conversation. Wherefore Tarquin, who at that time had only young children, became so attached to Servius, that he was generally thought to be his son; and with great pains instructed him in all those arts, which he 104himself had been taught, after the very superior manner of the Greeks. But when Tarquin had perished by the plots of the sons of Ancus, Servius, as I before said, began to reign, not by the command, but by the assent and sufferance of the people. For when Tarquin was falsely said to be alive, and sick from the effects of his wound; he declared the law in royal pomp, and discharged debtors with his own money. Conducting himself with much courtesy, he declared that he pronounced the law at the command of Tarquin. He did not commit himself to the fathers, but Tarquin being buried, he conferred with the people about himself, and being authorised to reign, he had his accession confirmed by a law of the curia. And first he avenged himself by war, for injuries received from the Etruscans, * * * * * *

[Two pages wanting.]

XXII. * * he inscribed eighteen centuries of horse in the great register. Afterwards having set apart a great number of equestrians from the mass of the whole people, he distributed the rest of the citizens into five classes, and divided the old from the young: and classed them in such a manner, that the suffrages were not in the power of the multitude, but of the landed proprietors. He was careful of what ought always to be observed in government; that numbers alone should not have the ascendency. Which classification if it were unknown to you, should be explained by me. You will perceive the plan was such, that the centuries of horse 105with six suffrages, (a century being added from the carpenters on account of their great utility to the city,) and the first class, make eighty-nine centuries: to which from the one hundred and four centuries, for so many remain; if only eight are added, the whole power of the people is obtained: and the much greater multitude comprehended in the ninety-six centuries remaining, is neither excluded from voting, lest it should seem disdainful; nor is it made too effective, lest it should be dangerous. In the which matter he was very circumspect even as to terms and names. Those from among the wealthy he called "assiduos"[15] from paying their taxes in money. Those who possessed no more than one thousand five hundred pieces of brass, or those who were polled in the register without any possessions whatever, he called proletaries; as if progeny only; that is, as if nothing but population might be expected from them. But of those ninety six centuries, more were enumerated in one century, than almost in the whole first class. Thus the right of suffrage was not prohibited to any one by law, and that class had a greater weight of suffrage, which had most at stake in the preservation of good government. As to public criers, men hired for parade, clarion players, horn players, and proletaries, * * * *

[Four pages wanting.]

XXIII. * * * * * Was[16] sixty-five years more ancient, being built thirty-nine years before the 106first olympiad. And the very ancient Lycurgus had the same thing in view. This equality therefore, and this triple nature of public affairs appears to me to have been common to us and to those people. But what is peculiar in our republic, and than which nothing can be more admirable, I will look very critically into if I am able; as nothing similar is to be found in any government. For these things which I have adverted to, were so mingled in this state, and among the Lacedemonians, and the Carthagenians, that they were not properly balanced. For in whatever government any one man enjoys perpetual power, especially royalty, although even a Senate may exist in it, as was the case at Rome under the kings, and in the laws of Lycurgus at Sparta; and even granting the people some share in the government, as was the fact under our kings: still that royal name will stand pre-eminent, nor can a government of that kind be any thing but a kingdom, or be called otherwise. But such a form of government is especially subject to change for this reason; that it easily falls into the most unprofitable courses, precipitated thereunto by the vices of one man. For the royal form of government itself, not only is not to be condemned, but I know not whether it is not greatly to be preferred to the other simple forms, if I could approve of any simple form of government. But only as long as it preserves its proper character, which is that the safety, the equality, and tranquillity of the citizens, are to be preserved by the justice, the wisdom, and the perpetual power of one man. Many things however are altogether wanting to a people subject to a king. 107Liberty among the first: which is not that we may live under a just master, but under none at all. * * *

[Two pages wanting.]
XXIV. For some time fortune prosperously accompanied this unjust and cruel master in the administration of affairs. He subdued all Latium in war, and took Suessa, an opulent and well stored Pometian city. Enriched with great spoils of gold and silver, he accomplished the vow of his ancestor in the building of the capitol. He established colonies, and according to the institutions of those from whom he had derived his origin, he sent magnificent gifts, as offerings of his spoils, to Apollo at Delphos.

XXV. Here the very circle is set in motion, whose natural movement and revolution you learn to distinguish from the beginning. For the very head of discretion in civil matters, upon which all our discourse turns, is to observe the ways and bendings of public affairs; so that when you perceive what way any thing inclines, you may either keep it back, or meet it by opposing other things to it. For the king of whom I speak, having stained himself first with the murder of a good king, no longer preserved his integrity of mind, and wished to inspire fear himself, because he dreaded every sort of punishment for his wickedness. Afterwards borne up with his victories and riches, he exulted with insolence, and imposed no restraint on his own conduct, or the licentiousness of his followers. Wherefore when his eldest son had used violence with Lucretia, 108the wife of Collatinus, and daughter of Tricipitinus, and the noble and chaste woman had inflicted death upon herself on account of that injury; L. Brutus, a man pre-eminent in mind and courage, released his fellow citizens from that unjust yoke of a cruel slavery: who, although he was a private citizen, sustained the whole government, and was the first who taught in this city, that no man was to be considered insignificant, when the public liberties were to be preserved. Under which leader and head, the whole city being in commotion, as well with the recent complaints of the family and kindred of Lucretia, as with the remembrance of the many wrongs done by the haughtiness of Tarquin himself, and his sons; the banishment of the king, his children, and his whole race was pronounced.

XXVI. Do not you perceive then how a master may spring out of a king, and how a form of government from being good, may become the very worst, through the vice of one man. This is that master over the people, whom the Greeks call tyrant; him only they esteem a king, who consults like a parent with the people, and preserves those over whom he is placed, in the most prosperous condition of life. A sort of government very good as I have said, but bordering upon and inclining to a very pernicious one. For when this king deviates into unjust rule, at once he becomes a tyrant, and an animal more hideous, more destructive, and more odious, in the eyes of gods and men cannot be conceived: surpassing, although in the human form, the most monstrous wild beasts in cruelty. How can he be rightly called a man, who observes no fellowship 109of humanity with his fellow citizens, no communion of law with the whole race of man? But a more proper place to speak of this will occur, when circumstances will suggest to us to speak of those, who have sought to usurp the Government over free cities.

XXVII. You have here then the origin of a tyrant, for the Greeks would have this to be the name of an unjust king. Our ancestors indeed have called all who have had an exclusive and perpetual dominion over the people, kings. Thus Spurius Cassius, M. Manilius, and Spurius Mælius, are said to have wished to establish a kingdom, and even * * * * * *

[Two pages wanting.]
XXVIII. Lycurgus gave the name of ancients[17] at Lacedemon, to that too small number of twenty-eight, to whom he wished the whole authority of counsel to be confided, while the sole command should be held by the king. Wherefore our ancestors translating and adopting that term, those whom he called ancients, they called a senate: as we have already stated Romulus to have done with the select fathers. Nevertheless, the royal title, and its strength and power were always pre-eminent. Impart too something of power to the people, as was done by Lycurgus and Romulus, and you will not satisfy them with freedom, but you will inflame them with the passion of liberty, when you have only permitted them to taste of power. The fear indeed 110will always hang over them, lest they should have an unjust king, which generally happens. The fortune therefore of a people is, as I said before, very uncertain, which is placed in the will or conduct of one man.

XXIX. Wherefore this first form, example, and origin of a tyrant, is found by us in that very government which Romulus instituted with auspices, and not in that, which Plato says Socrates imagined to himself in that peripatetic discourse. And as Tarquin subverted the whole fabric of royalty, not because he grasped a new sort of authority, but because he made a bad use of it; so let us oppose to him another; a good man, wise and expert in every thing useful and dignified in civil life: a tutor and steward as it were of the commonwealth, for so may be called whoever is the ruler and governor of a state. Imagine to yourselves that you recognise such a man; one who can protect the state, both by his counsel and conduct. And since the name of such a man has not been alluded to in this discourse, and that a character of this kind will be frequently treated of in what remains to be said * * * * * *

[Twelve pages wanting.]
XXX. * * * * * * Plato described a state more to be desired, than to be hoped for upon the smallest scale. He did not constitute things as they might exist, but in such a manner as the nature of civil affairs might be considered. As to myself, if in any way I am able to accomplish it, with the same principles which he had in view, I will look, not into the picture 111and shadow of a state, but into a most powerful republic; that I may appear to touch, as it were, the true cause of every public good and evil. After these two hundred and forty years of regal government, and indeed a little more, including the interregnums, Tarquin being banished, the royal title was as odious to the Roman people, as it had been regretted after the death, or rather the disappearance of Romulus, and as much as they wanted a king then, in like manner, after the expulsion of Tarquin, they could not endure the name of one.

XXXI. Under this feeling our ancestors then expelled Collatinus, who was innocent, through apprehension of his family connexions, and the other Tarquins from disgust at their names. From the same cause too P. Valerius ordered the fasces to be lowered when he began to speak before the people; and had his building materials taken to the foot of the Velia, as soon as he perceived the suspicions of the people to be raised on account of his having begun to build in a more conspicuous part of the Velia, the very place where King Tullus had dwelt. He also, in the which he greatly deserved the name of Publicola, had that law passed for the people, which was first carried in the meetings of the centuries, that no unfriendly magistrate should put to death, or flog any Roman citizen for appealing. The pontifical books however declare appeals to have existed under the kings; the augural records show it also. The twelve tables too in many laws indicate that it was lawful to appeal from every judgment and punishment. What is brought down to us by tradition, of the Decemvirs 112who wrote the laws, being created without any appeal, sufficiently shows that the other magistrates had not the power of judging without appeal. The law, too, which for the sake of concord passed in the consulate of Lucius Valerius Potitus, and M. Horatius Barbatus, men very justly popular; sanctioned the principle, that no magistrate should be created without appeal. Nor did the Portian laws, which are three as you know of the three Portii, contain any thing new except the confirmation of it. Publicola therefore, upon the law in favour of appeal being published, immediately ordered the axes to be taken from off the fasces, and the next day had Sp. Lucretius appointed to him as his colleague: being his superior in age, he ordered his own lictors to go to him; and first established the custom that lictors should precede each of the consuls, alternate months, lest the ensigns of command among a free people, should be as numerous as in a kingdom. There was something more than mediocrity in this man, as I consider him: who having given a moderate liberty to the people, preserved more easily the authority of the chiefs. Nor do I repeat these things, now so old and obsolete to you, without cause. I select examples of men and things drawn from illustrious persons and times, to which the remainder of my discourse shall be applied.

XXXII. In such a manner the senate governed the commonwealth in those days, that though the people were free, still they interfered in but few things. Public affairs were principally managed under the authority, and by the rules and customs of the senate. And although the consuls possessed their power only for a 113year, it was royal in its nature and effect. And this was strenuously preserved, as necessary to the preservation of the influence of the nobles and principal chiefs, that nothing should be established in the meetings of the people, which was not sanctioned by the authority of the fathers. In these very times too, T. Larcius was appointed dictator, about ten years after the first consuls. A new kind of authority, very much resembling, as we perceive, the royal power. But all great matters were conducted by the authority of the principal men, the people submitting to it. And great events took place in those times in war, under renowned men in the supreme command, from among those very dictators and consuls.

XXXIII. But what belongs to the very nature of things, as that a people emancipated from kings, should take a little more power to themselves; was brought about not long after, about the sixteenth year, in the consulate of Postumus Cominus, and Sp. Cassius. Not in the right way perhaps, but it is of the nature of public affairs frequently to deviate from what is right. For observe what I said in the beginning, that unless an equable compensation prevails in a state, in the laws, in offices, in emoluments; so that the magistrates enjoy their proper degree of power; the chief men their authority in council, and the people their liberties, such a state of the government cannot remain unchanged. For when the city was in commotion on account of the pressure of their debts, the people first occupied the Sacred Mount, then the Aventine. Nor could the discipline even of Lycurgus keep the Greeks 114within those restraints. In the reign of Theopompus, at Sparta, those five whom they call Ephori; the ten too in Crete, who are called Cosmoi; arose against the royal power, as the tribunes of the people did against the consular authority.

XXXIV. Perhaps there was a mode by which our ancestors might have relieved the pressure of the law of debt, which had not escaped Solon, the Athenian, some short time before, and which our senate adopted not long after, when on account of the infamous conduct of a creditor, the citizens were liberated from the general oppression, and voluntary bondage on account of debt abolished in future.[18] And always at such periods, 115when the common people are exhausted by contributions in times of public calamity, some relief and remedy is to be devised for the common safety. Which the senate having neglected to do, sufficient cause was given to the people to create two tribunes during a sedition of the plebeians, with intent to weaken the power and authority of the senate; which nevertheless remained a grave and great body, bringing forward in the service of the state the wisest and bravest men, and strengthening it by arms and counsel. And their authority was the greater, because far excelling all others in honour, they were less conspicuous for voluptuousness, and not much signalized by their wealth. Their high worth also was the more esteemed in the state, because in private life they diligently assisted individuals by their advice, and by substantial services.

116XXXV. In which situation of the republic, the quæstor accused Sp. Cassius, who enjoyed the highest degree of favour with the people, and was contriving a usurpation of the government; and as you have heard, when his own father stated himself to be satisfied of his guilt, the people assenting to it, he put him to death. It was a grateful thing also to the people, when Sp. Tarpeius, and A. Aternius, consuls, about fifty-four years after the first consuls, carried a law in the meetings of the centuries concerning fines. Twenty years afterwards when L. Papirius, and P. Pinarius, censors, by pronouncing fines, converted the strength of the flocks of many private individuals to the public use; a light valuation of cattle was ordained in the law on fines, during the consulate of C. Julius and P. Papirius.

XXXVI. But some years before, when the senate enjoyed the greatest authority, the people being very patient and obedient, a new plan was instituted. The consuls and the tribunes of the people abdicated the magistracy, and ten men were created with the greatest authority, and without appeal, who were to possess the supreme power, and to inscribe the laws. Who when they with great equity and prudence, had written ten tables of laws, appointed ten other decemvirs for the following year, whose faith and justice are not in like manner praised. From which college, however, comes that praiseworthy act of C. Julius, who stated that in his presence a body had been dug out of the chamber of a patrician, L. Sestius. Although he had supreme power, and as decemvir was without appeal, he admitted him to bail, refusing to lose sight of that most excellent 117law, which forbids sentence to be pronounced on the head of a Roman citizen, unless in the meetings of the centuries.

XXXVII. A third decemviral year followed under the same men, they being unwilling to appoint others. In this condition of the commonwealth, which I have often already stated not to be lasting, because it is not equable to all the orders of the state, the chief men had the whole government in their hands; the most noble decemvirs being always preferred. No tribunes of plebeians opposed to them, no other magistrates associated with them, and no appeal left to the people against death and stripes. Wherefore on account of the injustice of these men, a great disturbance suddenly arose, and a revolution took place in the whole commonwealth. They added two tables of iniquitous laws, in which the very marriages which were even permitted to strangers, were forbidden by an inhuman law, lest the plebeians should connect themselves with the fathers; which law was afterwards abrogated by the plebicist Canuleius. In all things they conducted themselves libidinously, cruelly, and avariciously towards the people. Upon that celebrated and well known affair contained in many literary records, in which one Decimus Virginius on account of the outrage of one of the decemvirs, slew his virgin daughter with his own hand in the Forum, and fled lamenting to the army which was then on Mount Algide; the soldiers abandoned the war they were then engaged in, and as was before done for a similar cause, first came to the sacred mount, and next to the Aventine * * * * *

118[Eight pages wanting.]
XXXVIII. When Scipio had spoken these things, and all by their silence were expecting the remainder.—"Since my seniors here, Africanus," said Tubero, "ask you no questions, hear from me what I still find wanting in your discourse." "Most cheerfully," replied Scipio. "You appear to me," said he "to have been pronouncing the eulogium of our republic, when Lælius was inquiring not respecting ours, but of government in general. Nor have I learnt from your discourse, by what discipline, or by what customs or laws, a republic like the one you praise, can be constituted or preserved."

XXXIX. "I think," said Africanus, "we shall by and by have a more appropriate occasion, Tubero, of discussing the establishment and preservation of states. In respect to the best kind of government, I deem myself to have sufficiently answered the inquiries which Lælius made. First I pointed out three kinds of government that might be endured, and to these three their very pernicious opposites: that no one among them was the best, but that one moderately balanced from all three, was preferable to either of them. That I have availed myself of our state for an example, was not with a view to define the best form of government, for that could be done without an example. But in truth, that a great state might present the very picture, such as reason and language might describe it to be. But if without going to the example of any people, you are desirous of finding 119that perfect condition of government, then look at the image which nature presents to us * * *

[A great number of pages wanting here.]
XL. S. * * * a character I have been looking for, and have been desirous of arriving at.

L. The discreet statesman, perhaps?

S. The very same.

L. You have all those present who are so numerous: or you can begin with yourself. "I wish," said Scipio, "it was proportionally so in the whole senate. However, he is a discreet man, who as we have frequently seen in Africa, seated on a monstrous wild and ferocious animal, governs and directs him; making him kneel down, not with blows, but with a slight sign."

45

L. I know, and have often seen it when I was Lieutenant to you.

S. So the Indian or Carthagenian governs a wild beast, and renders it docile and gentle with humane conduct. But that intellectual principle which is hidden in the souls of men, and which is called a part of the soul, does not bridle or tame one easily subdued, whenever it accomplishes it, which rarely happens. For that ferocious animal must be restrained[19] * * * *

[Either four or eight pages are wanting here.]
120XLII. "Already," said Lælius, "I see the man I expected, so greatly endowed, and charged with such duties." "With this duty only," replied Africanus, "for in this one almost all the rest are included. That in his thoughts and actions he never deviate from himself, so that he may call upon others to imitate him, and that he may offer himself in the purity of his mind and his life, as a mirror to his fellow citizens. For as in stringed instruments or pipes, as well as in singing with voices, a certain harmony is to be formed with distinct sounds, an interruption to which cannot be borne by refined ears; this kindred and harmonious concert being produced by the modification of dissimilar voices. So a government temperately organized from the upper, the lower and middle orders blended together, harmonizes like music by the agreement of dissimilar sounds. And that which in song is called by musicians, harmony, is concord in a state; the strongest and best bond of safety in every republic; yet which without justice cannot be preserved.[20]

[Many pages wanting.]
121XLIV. "I assent entirely to it," said Scipio, "and declare freely to you, that we must esteem in nothing all that we have said upon government, or that may remain farther to be said, unless it be established, not only that it is false, that injustice is necessary, but that this is most true; that without the most perfect justice, no government can prosper in any manner. But if you please, thus far for to day. The remainder, for many things remain yet to be said, we will defer until to-morrow." When this was approved, an end was put to the discussion for that day.

12. 122Pecuniosi.

13. Locupletes.

14. Plato.

15. Asses dare.

16. Carthage.

17. γèροντας in the MSS.

18. This passage appears to deserve a note. The words "nexa" and "nectier" are used in the original. And at the first glance, the passage, connecting it with the well known custom of keeping debtors in chains, as well as the memorable occasion which produced this insurrectionary movement, would appear to declare, that all kinds of bondage for debt were abolished in future. In early periods, whoever was unable to pay his debts, was

adjudged by a decree of the prætor, to discharge them in personal services: for which purpose his person was delivered to his creditor; whose slave in every sense of the word he thus became, until the debt was discharged. A debtor thus situated was termed "addictus" or sentenced. Livy, vi. 36., relates "that those against whom judgments had been given, (addictos) were led out daily in herds from the Forum, to the mansions of the patricians, which were filled with enchained debtors: and that wherever a patrician dwelt, there was a private prison." That all debtors were subject to actual bonds, appears from every indebted person under voluntary judgment, being called "nexus," meaning linked or chained; and probably when judgment was passed, debtors were delivered in that condition to the creditors. But "nexus" changed its meaning, as the word "bond" has done in our language, where we bind ourselves only with forms. The urgent necessity of the plebeians, arising out of the exactions of the patricians, obliged them to borrow money at usury; and upon such occasions, for money weighed out to him "per æs et libram," before witnesses, the borrower pledged his person and liberty to the lender as security for the debt. This voluntary act, which was equivalent to a modern confession of judgment, constituted the debtor a "nexus;" before the period of payment had expired, at which time only he was liable to fetters. Upon the occasion of the insurrection mentioned in the passage; a young man of respectable plebeian family, C. Publilius, surrendered himself to Papirius, a patrician usurer, in the place of his father who had failed to redeem himself from his "nexus." Rejecting the infamous propositions made to him, Papirius caused him to be cruelly scourged. This transaction having roused the people, the senate was obliged to consent to the liberation of all persons who had become "nexi" by their voluntary act, and to order the practice to be discontinued in future.

I have translated the passage in accordance with this view of the subject. Niebuhr, vol. i. 506. Livy, vi. 36. viii. 28. &c.

19. The continuation of this passage is, perhaps, found in Nonius Voc. Exsultare, "which nourishes itself with blood, and which so delights in every kind of cruelty, that it scarcely can be satiated with the sad destruction of human beings."

20. Professor Mai quotes the following passage from St. Augustin, De. Civ. Dei, as containing a summary of that part of the discussion interrupted here. "And when Scipio had in a more comprehensive and diffuse way, shown how advantageous justice was to a state, and how injurious the absence of it was: Philus, who was one of those present at the discussion, took it up, and proposed that that subject should be very carefully investigated, on account of the opinion which was obtaining, that governments could not be administered without injustice."

123
CICERO'S REPUBLIC.

BOOK III.

[Four or eight pages wanting.]
II. * * * * The intelligent principle having found man endowed with the faculty of uttering rude and imperfect sounds, enabled him to separate and distinguish them into articulations. Thus words were affixed to things as signs of them, and man, once solitary, became united to man, by the sweet bond of conversation. By the same intelligence, the

inflexions of the voice, which we find to be infinite in number, are all distinguished and expressed, by the invention of a few marks, which enable us to hold a correspondence with the absent, to indicate our inclinations, and to preserve a record of things past. To this the knowledge of numbers was added, a thing not only necessary to life, but at once immutable and eternal. Which first led us to consider the heavens, to look upon the motion of the planets with interest, and the numbering of the nights and days * * * *

[Eight or ten pages wanting.]
124III. * * * * Whose minds rose to a loftier pitch as I before said, that they might execute or discover something worthy of the gift they had received from the gods. Wherefore let those who have treated upon the moral conduct of life, be deemed by us, great men, as they are; learned men; masters of truth and virtue. Yet let it be admitted that civil rights, and the government of a people, whether they are the fruits of men experienced in the management of public affairs, or, as the fact has been, the result of their literary leisure, be least despised; causing as they do to spring up in great minds, as we have often seen, an incredible and divine virtue. For if any one to those faculties which the mind has from nature, and to those talents which civil institutions produce, hath added also the learning, and the more various knowledge of things, in which men engaged in the discussion of those books are versed, there is no one who ought not to prefer such a man to all others. For what can be more excellent, than when the practice and habit of great affairs is joined to a perfect knowledge of the theory of the science of them? Or what more perfect can be imagined than P. Scipio, C. Lælius, and L. Philus; who that they might omit nothing appertaining to the high character of enlightened men, to the knowledge of our domestic and ancient customs, united the learning received from Socrates? Wherefore he who determined and effected both, that is, instructed himself as well in the institutions, as in the philosophy of the ancients, I think has accomplished every thing with praise. But if a choice must be made between those two paths to excellence, 125and if to any one, that tranquil way of life passed in the best studies and sciences may appear happier, still certainly an active, civil life is more illustrious and more laudable. The greatest men derive their glory from such a life, as M. Curius * * * *

"Whom none could overcome with arms or gold."
[Six pages wanting.]
IV. * * * Nevertheless this difference existed in their two different modes: the one unfolded the principles of nature by their studies and by their eloquence; the others by their institutions and by their laws. This commonwealth alone has produced many, if not altogether to be deemed sages, since that title is so cautiously bestowed, yet worthy of the greatest praise; for they cultivated the precepts and discoveries of sages. Wherefore civil governments are to be extolled and ever will be, since in the nature of things, to constitute a commonwealth which shall be lasting, is one of the greatest efforts of mind: and thus if we only enumerate one for every country, what a multitude of excellent men do we find. For if we permit our minds to take a survey of that famous Greece, of Italy, Latium, or the Sabine and Volscian people; the Samnites, the Etrurians; next the Assyrians, the Persians, the Carthagenians. If these * * *

[Twelve pages wanting.]
V. * * * "Truly," said Philus, "you have 126imposed a fine task upon me, wishing me to undertake the justification of what is wrong." "Surely," said Lælius, "you are afraid lest in using the same arguments which are wont to be brought forward against justice, you may

appear to hold such opinions yourself; you who are almost the only example left of ancient probity and faith. But your habit of discussing both sides of the question, in order more easily to get at the truth, is very well known." "Well, well," said Philus, "I will do as you wish, and defile myself with my eyes open: for since those who search for gold do not refuse to do it; we who are looking for what is right, a thing much more precious than gold, assuredly ought not to avoid any thing that is disagreeable. And I wish, since I am about to make use of another man's opinions, it was possible for me to make use of his tongue also. Now, however, L. Furius Philus, must say what Carneades, a Greek in the habit of saying whatever he pleased * * *

[Four pages wanting.]
VIII. * * * But the other has filled four pretty large books with the subject of justice. From Chrysippus I have never looked for any thing very great or magnificent; since he reasons in a particular way of his own, and examines things rather by the force of words, than the weight of facts. It was for those distinguished men, to raise up that prostrate virtue, and elevate it to the divine heights of wisdom. A virtue which stands alone as it were, greatly munificent and 127liberal; which loves every thing better than itself, and is born more for others, than for its own interests. Nor was the inclination wanting to them: for what other cause had they for writing, or what motive soever? In genius they excelled all. But the cause was greater even than their inclination and strength. The right indeed concerning which we inquire, is something civil, not natural: if it were, justice and injustice would be the same things to all men, as hot and cold, bitter and sweet things are.

IX. Now however, if any one borne upon the chariot with winged serpents, of which Pacuvius speaks, could survey with his eyes, and look down upon the many and various nations and cities; he might see chiefly among that unchanging race of the Egyptians, which preserves in its records the memory of so many events and ages, an ox esteemed as a god, which the Egyptians call Apis; and many other strange things among them, among which wild beasts consecrated into the number of the gods. Then in Greece, where as with us, magnificent temples are consecrated containing human images, which the Persians considered impious. For which cause alone, Xerxes is said to have ordered the temples of the Athenians to be burnt; considering it to be wicked to shut the gods up within walls, whose residence was the whole universe. Afterwards Philip who had it in contemplation, and Alexander who carried it into effect, gave as reasons for making war against the Persians, that they avenged the temples of Greece; which the Greeks did not think of repairing, that the devastation might be an eternal monument to 128posterity of the infamy of the Persians. How many, as the Taurians in Axinum, as Busiris the king of Egypt, as the Gauls, the Carthagenians, have thought it a grateful and pious duty to the gods, to immolate men. But the institutions of life differ so much, that the Cretans and Etolians esteem it honourable to steal: the Lacedemonians used to say that all lands were theirs which they could reach with a shaft. The Athenians were wont to swear even publicly, that every soil was theirs, which produced oil and corn. The Gauls consider it shameful to produce grain by labour, and therefore go armed to harvest other people's lands. But we, the most just of men, to make our own olive and vineyards more valuable, do not permit the transalpine nations to plant them: in doing which we are said to act prudently; it is not called acting justly. By which you may understand there is a wide distance between prudence and equity. Lycurgus, the founder of the best laws, and the most equal rights, gave the lands of the wealthy to be cultivated by the lower class in the state of servitude.

X. But if I were to describe the various kinds of laws, of institutions, of customs and manners, not only so different among such divers nations, but even in a single city, or in this, I could demonstrate them to have been changed a thousand times. Our friend Manilius here, an interpreter of laws, will tell you that other laws exist now concerning the legacies and inheritances of women, than those he was wont to speak of in his youth, before the Voconian law was passed; which very law, indeed proposed for the advantage of the men, is full 129of injustice towards the women. For why should a woman not have possessions? Why should a vestal appoint an heir, and her mother not? Why if limits were to be put to the possessions of women, should the daughter of Crassus, if she were an only daughter, possess thousands legally, when mine could not possess two or three hundred * * * * * *

[Two pages wanting.]
XI. * * * * * * If these rights were thus sanctioned in us, all men would have the same rights, and would not have different rights at different periods. But if it is the duty of a just and good man to obey the laws, I would ask which are they to be? Or shall he obey all indiscriminately? But virtue does not admit of uncertainty, nor nature endure inconstancy. The strength of law consists in punishment, not in our natural justice. Natural right therefore does not exist. Whence it follows, that men are not made just by nature. But it is said, although there are various laws, still good men, by natural inclination, pursue what is just in itself, and not what is assumed to be so; because it is the part of a good and just man, to render that justice to every one which he is deserving of. Now, first, are we in any wise just to the dumb beasts? For men, not of mediocrity, but great and learned; Pythagoras and Empedocles, declare that all animals possess the same degree of right, and denounce unatoning punishments to hang over those by whom any 130animal is outraged. It is wicked therefore to injure the brutes. * * * * * *

[Eight pages wanting.]
XII. * * * * * * what we call wisdom, urges us to increase our wealth, our riches, and to extend our possessions. How could that great commander[21] who formerly carried the limits of his empire into Asia; how could he govern, bear sway, reign, have dominion, and the full enjoyment of voluptuousness, unless he took something from others? But justice orders us to spare all, to consult the welfare of mankind, to give to every one his own, and to abstain from every thing that is sacred, every thing that is public, every thing which is not our own. What therefore is to be done? If wisdom is consulted, riches, power, wealth, honours, authority, empire, are open to individuals and nations. But since it is the public interest we are discussing, instances of a public nature will illustrate better; and as the same degree of right is in both, I shall advert to the wisdom of a nation, and I shall omit the rest. Our own nation, which Africanus in his discourse yesterday, traced to its origin, whose empire already extends over the earth, has it, once least of them all, become so by justice or wisdom? * * * * * *

[Four or eight pages wanting.]
XIV. For all who possess the power of life and death over a people are tyrants, yet they prefer to be 131called kings by the name of the good Jupiter. When certain persons through the influence of their riches, their class, or other circumstances, possess themselves of the government, it is a faction. Yet they call themselves, the better class. If the people however are uppermost and rule every thing at their own pleasure, that is

called liberty; nevertheless it is licentiousness. But when one fears another, man mistrusting man, and one class another, then because no one confides, a sort of pact is made between the people and the great, from whence that combined form of government springs, which Scipio has praised. So that neither nature, or the will is the mother of justice, but weakness. For when one thing is to be chosen out of three, either to do injustice without permitting it to be done to you; or to do it and permit it also; or neither one or the other: the best is to do it with impunity[22] if you can; the second best is neither to do it, nor suffer it to be done to you: the worst of all is to be eternally fighting now on account of your own aggressions, now on account of those of others * * * * *

[An unknown number of pages wanting.]
* * * Except the Arcadians and the Athenians, who, I suppose, fearing lest at some period this decree[23] of justice might appear, have feigned themselves to be sprung from the earth, like the little mice we see in the fields.

XVI. To these things, others are wont to be added principally by those, distinguished for their honesty in discussion, and having more weight for that reason. Who when engaged in the inquiry of what constitutes a good man, frank and plain as we wish to find him, are not themselves crafty, hardened, and malicious in argument. They deny that the wise man is good only because goodness and justice are pleasing to him from their nature; but because the lives of good men are free from apprehension, care, solicitude and danger. Whereas bad men have always a sting goading their souls, and judgment and punishment are always present to their eyes. That there is no emolument, no advantage arising from injustice, so great as to compensate the fear, and the constant thought that some punishment is impending * * * * *

[Four or eight pages wanting.]
XVII. I ask if there be two men, one of them of the very best kind; equitable, perfectly just, of exemplary faith: the other singular for his wickedness and audacity: and suppose the community in such an error, that the good man passes for a wicked and dishonest one; while the bad one has the reputation of perfect probity and good faith. And through this general delusion of the citizens, the good man is harassed, arrested, bound, his eyes put out, condemned, thrown in chains, tortured in the fire, banished. Wanting every thing, at last he appears to all to be deservedly the most wretched of men. On the other hand, the bad man is praised, sought after, caressed by all. Honours of every kind, authority, power, and every advantage conferred upon him from all sides. A man, finally, in the estimation of all deemed the very best, and worthy of the highest gifts of fortune. Who would be so insane as to hesitate which of these two he would choose to be?

XVIII. As it is with individuals, so it is with nations. No community is so stupid, as not to prefer commanding by injustice, to serving according to justice. I shall not go far back for examples. Being consul, you assisting me in council; I had to examine the Numantine treaty. Who is ignorant that Pompey made that treaty, and that Mancinus was concerned in the same affair? This last most excellent man supported the proposition I carried from the consultation in the senate; the other most earnestly opposed it. Those who valued modesty, integrity, and good faith preferred Mancinus: yet for his reasoning, counsel, and policy, Pompey took the lead of him * * * *

[An unknown number of pages wanting.]

XXIX. * * * * * Ti. Gracchus was vigilant for the interests of the people, but neglected the rights of the Latins and the treaties with the allies. If such customs and license should spread themselves wider, and our empire be changed from right to force, so that those who until now voluntarily obey us, should be ruled only by terror; although it has been vigilantly preserved for us, who are of the present age; yet I should be very solicitous about our posterity, and about the immortality of the republic, which might be perpetual, if the institutions and manners of our forefathers were preserved.

XXX. When Lælius had thus spoken, all present expressed themselves to have been very much delighted by him, but Scipio, among the rest, as if quite elated with pleasure, "many causes," said he, "indeed Lælius, hast thou often defended, in such a manner that I can by no means compare our colleague Servius Galba to thee; whom when he lived thou preferredest to all; nor in truth any of the attic orators * * *

[Twelve pages wanting.]

XXXI. * * * * * Therefore that common interest, that is the commonwealth, who can recognize it when all are oppressed by the cruelty of one; when no bond of Law exists, nor that consent of congregated society, which constitutes a people. And this very condition of the Syracusans: a celebrated city, as Timæus says, the first among the Greeks, and the most beautiful of them all: its harbour embosomed within the walls, its canals running through the city: its broad streets, its porticoes, temples, fortifications, all these did not help to constitute a commonwealth, while Dionysius reigned. The people had no part in them, for the very people belonged to one man. Therefore where there is a tyrant, it is not a vitiated commonwealth, as I said yesterday, but reason compels us to declare plainly that no commonwealth at all exists.

XXXII. "Indeed" said Lælius, "you speak very clearly, and I already perceive the drift of your discourse.

S. You see therefore, that when every thing is in the power of a faction, neither can that be properly called a commonwealth.

L. I judge it plainly so.

S. And most rightly do you judge, for what was the condition of the Athenians, when after that great Peloponesian war, thirty men were most unjustly placed in the command of that city? Did the ancient glory of the city, the admirable nature of its buildings, its theatre, gymnasia, its noble porticoes, its citadel, or the admirable works of Phidias, or the magnificent port of Piræus, did they constitute a commonwealth? "Not in the least" said Lælius, "because indeed the common interest was not thought of."

S. How was it at Rome, when the Decemvirs existed without appeal, in that third year, when liberty itself had parted with its privileges?

L. Nothing was left to the people, and truly it was necessary to bring them to that point, that they might recover their rights.

XXXIII. S. I come now to the third kind, that in which some inconsistency will perhaps be perceived, where all things are said to be done by the people, and to be in the power of the people. When the multitude orders punishments to be inflicted in any manner that it pleases, ordering, seizing, keeping, dissipating every thing whatever they choose, can you then Lælius, deny that to be a republic, where all things belong to the people, and when indeed we define a republic to be a commonwealth?" "There is nothing," said Lælius, "I would sooner deny to be a republic, than where all things are in the power of the multitude. We did not consider that they had a republic among the Syracusans, or at Agrigentum, or at Athens when they were under tyrants, or at Rome when under the decemvirs. Nor do I see how the name of republic is appropriate when the multitude rules. Because first, as you have happily defined it to me, Scipio, a people does not exist, but where it is held together by consent of law; and this sort of mob, is as much a tyrant as if it were one man. Indeed it is more mischievous, for nothing is more ferocious than the wild beast which assumes the name and form of the people. Nor is it right, when the property of maniacs is placed by law under the guardianship of kindred, that * * *

[Eight pages wanting.]

XXXIV. * * * of it,[24] it may with as much propriety be said that it is a republic and a commonwealth, as it may be said of a kingdom. "And much more," said Mummius, "for a king being one, is more like a master; but where many good men are at the head of affairs in a republic, nothing can be more happily constituted. But I certainly prefer a kingdom to the sway of a democracy; which third and most vicious kind of government remains for you to explain."

XXXV. To this Scipio replied, "I recognize well Spurius, your steady aversion to the popular mode, and although it might be treated with less aversion than you are wont to do, nevertheless I agree, that of all these three kinds, no one is less to be approved of. I do not however agree with you that the better class are to be preferred to a king; for if it is wisdom which governs a state, of what consequence is it, whether it resides in one, or in many? But in our discussion we are led into a sort of error. When we call them the better class, nothing can be conceived more excellent, for what can be imagined more desirable than the best? When however a king is mentioned, an unjust king occurs to our minds. We do not nevertheless intend to speak of an unjust king, in our examination of this royal kind of government. Think of Romulus, Pompilius, and Tullus as kings, and perhaps you will not be so displeased with that kind of government.

M. What sort of praise then is left for a democratic government?

S. What did you think, Spurius, of the Rhodians, with whom we were together; did you see nothing like a commonwealth there?

M. Indeed I did, and least of all to be blamed.

S. You say well. But if you remember all were alike; sometimes plebeians, sometimes senators; and by turns discharging during certain months their functions as senators; the other months they remained in the ranks of the people. In both capacities however they had the privilege of being present at the meetings for deliberation, and equally in the theatres and in the courts, great matters and all others were judged; so numerous was the multitude and so great its power that * * * * *

21. Alexander.

22. These are sophisms brought forward in favour of injustice.

Vide Lact. Inst. 5.
23. To restore things unjustly acquired.

24. The better class.

CICERO'S REPUBLIC.

BOOK IV.

II. * * * * * * How conveniently the orders are set down; the ages, the classes. The equestrian order where the senate votes. Too many foolishly seek to abolish that useful institution, hoping that through some Plebecists procuring the sale of the horses, they may get a largess.

III. Look now at the other provisions so wisely made, that the citizens may enjoy a happy and honest state of society, for that is the very motive for their union; and which government ought to secure to men, by institutions and laws. In the first place, as to puerile discipline for free-born young men, respecting which the Greeks have laboured so much in vain; and the only matter about which our guest Polybius reproaches the negligence of our institutions. No defined system, or of a public nature, or uniform for all, was decreed by the laws.

[Four or eight pages wanting.]
IV. * * * * * * nor naked when at an age of puberty. So deep did they seek as it were to lay the foundations of modesty. But how absurd the exercises of youth in the Grecian Gymnasia; how trifling that drilling of young boys: what loose and unrestrained manners permitted to them. I say nothing of the Eleans and Thebans, among whom free license and permission was given to the young people to indulge in sensuality. The Lacedemonians too, when they allowed every sensual indulgence short of violence, among their youth, were destroying what they were granting such a slight protection to. "I clearly understand, Scipio," said Lælius, "that in these practices of the Greeks, which you reprehend, you had rather attack the most illustrious people, than your favourite Plato, whom you do not assail at all, especially * * * * *

CICERO'S REPUBLIC.

BOOK V.

II. * * * * * * No prerogative more royal than the administration of justice, in which was comprehended the expounding of rights, for individuals were accustomed to seek justice from kings. On which account the lands, the fields, the groves, the extensive and rich grazing districts were defined, which belonged to the sovereign, and were all managed without any care or labour on his part; that none of the cares of private business, might abstract him from the affairs of the public. Nor was any man an umpire or arbitrator of any legal contention, but all things were decided by royal judgments. And it seems to me, that our Numa chiefly adopted this ancient custom from the kings of Greece. For the others, although they also discharged this function, yet a great many of them waged wars, and occupied themselves in establishing the rules of war. But that long peace of Numa, was the parent of law and religion to this city. He also was the writer of those laws which you know to be extant: all which is appropriate to the very citizen whose character we are drawing * * * * * *

142[An unknown number of pages wanting.]
III. S. Do you think there is any harm in his being acquainted with the nature of roots and seeds?

M. None, if only his work is not neglected.

S. But do you think it to be properly the study of a farmer?

M. Not in the least; for the cultivation of the land would often be unattended to.

S. Therefore, as a farmer is acquainted with the nature of his soil, a steward with the nature of letters, and each can turn from the amusement of theory to the greater utility of practice; so this our ruler may be thoroughly conversant with the knowledge of rights and of laws; he may have looked even into the very fountains of them: but let not his consultations, his constant readings, and his writings occupy him too much; but let him be as it were both steward and farmer to the commonwealth. Let him be skilled in the principles of law without which no man can be just; let him not be ignorant of civil law: but let it be as the pilot who studies the stars; the physician who studies the nature of plants and minerals; each turning his knowledge to the benefit of his art, without permitting it to impede the practical use of his vocation * * *

[An unknown number of pages wanting.]
IV. * * * * In those states where the good look for praise and honour, and fly from ignominy and disgrace. Not so much restrained by apprehension of 143the penalties established by law, but by a sentiment of self-respect, which nature has planted in man, a sort of dread of deserved censure. This sentiment the ruler of a state strengthens by public opinion, and confirms by education, and by institutions, that shame may deter the citizen from crime as much as fear. But these considerations properly belong to renown, and shall be more abundantly considered.

V. Life, however, and the comfortable enjoyment of it, are constituted by legal marriages, lawful children; the keeping hallowed the seats of the penate gods, and the domestic lares; that all may enjoy public and private comforts. Without good government, private life cannot be agreeable, nor can any one be more happy than in a well regulated state * * * *

Manufactured by Amazon.ca
Bolton, ON